W9-BGK-037

THE
QUEST FOR
KING
ARTHUR

DAVID DAY

De Agostini Editions

The Quest for King Arthur

For Stelios Platonos
Master Raconteur of the Parian Round Table

First published in Great Britain
by De Agostini Editions
Griffin House
161 Hammersmith Road
London W6 8SD

Copyright © 1995 De Agostini Editions Ltd
Text © David Day
Foreword © Terry Jones

All rights reserved.

No part of this work may be reproduced or utilized in
any form or by any means, electronic or mechanical,
including photocopying, recording or by any
information storage and retrieval system, without the
prior permission of the Publishers.

A CIP catalogue record for this book
is available from the British Library.

ISBN 1 899883 02 9

Printed in Italy
by Officine Grafiche De Agostini, Novara

CONTENTS

FOREWORD

For a historical figure, King Arthur seems remarkably fictional; yet for a fictional character he has had an extraordinary impact on the history of Britain.

David Day's fabulous new book about King Arthur disentangles the fiction from the history. I say "fabulous" because that is exactly what it is – it takes a tapestry of fables, sorts out the threads of truth and weaves them together into a vivid new picture.

When we were writing *Monty Python and the Holy Grail*, I remember being baffled in my attempts to pin down King Arthur into a single story that we could use as a basis for our film. Each account of him seemed to contradict another and the more I read the more confused I found myself. I wish David Day's book had been available then. Not only would it have put King Arthur into his historical perspective, but it would also have provided some hilarious material: like most history, much of King Arthur's story would fit easily into a Monty Python script. For example, it seems that there were two historical Arthurs and two Merlins and none of them knew each other. And although they are heroes of Anglo-Saxon and Norman England, most of them were actually Welsh-speaking Romanized Celts who lived in the lowlands of Scotland. What is more, none of them were really kings or wizards. Confused? Read on!

In the magical world of King Arthur, nothing is what it seems and everything transmutes into something else. Bits of Gawain turn up in a new incarnation as Lancelot. Arthur's own character as an implacable warrior undergoes a sea-change at the hands of French love-song lyricists, and the Lady of the Lake turns out to originate in a tribe of Greek lake nymphs. Even once perfectly respectable ladies like Morgan Le Fay and Guinevere metamorphize into a wicked fairy and a scheming harlot at the hands of a group of misogynistic twelfth-century monks, who seriously debated whether or not women had souls!

The first full account of King Arthur's life and times is found in *The History of the Kings of Britain*, written by Geoffrey of Monmouth in 1136. This "bizarre combination of fact and fiction that has and will forever inspire, baffle and enrage its readers" has nonetheless, according to David Day, "proved to be one of the most influential books in the whole of European history." Its account of King Arthur's life has been manipulated by almost every British sovereign to prove his or her right to rule, and it was used as the factual and legal basis for five centuries of war between France and Britain. Python has had no monopoly of the absurd.

Ever since Malory's *Morte d'Arthur* was published in 1485, the Arthurian legends have all too often been isolated in the realm of literature. The great strength of this book is that it places them in the real world in which and for which they were created. Many disparate strands are here pulled together for the first time. David Day applies his eclectic knowledge of mythology, linguistics, totemic language, symbolism, heraldry, alchemy and even metallurgy to provide new insights into the world of the Round Table, bringing the Arthurian legends to life in a quite extraordinary way. *The Quest for King Arthur* is the most enlightening single text on King Arthur to have been written since Malory first laid his hero to rest.

Terry Jones, London, 1995.

CHAPTER ONE

THE COMING OF ARTHUR

Arthur gathered together what warriors there were in the island of
Britain...and at his coming there was great fear and trembling.
The Mabinogion – *Anon*

A cyclone. That is what King Arthur most resembles. A whirlwind that constantly changes shape and moves. It picks up fragments wherever it goes and they all become part of the whirling entity we call a cyclone. There is little doubt that the being we call King Arthur once existed. Indeed, for most people he still exists and always will. But if we are searching for the real historical Arthur – or the accumulative King Arthur – we must do a little work. The real King Arthur is like the cyclone's eye: still and silent and invisible. We can only perceive him by the turbulence around him. There is a titanic cyclone of history, myth, legend, fantasy and romance whirling about King Arthur. Only a handful of figures in history have created so much turbulence. Why Arthur?

The great Argentinean writer Jorge Luis Borges once observed that nearly all civilizations created stories with dragons in them. Although he could no more explain a dragon than he could explain the universe, he believed that psychologically, sociologically and imaginatively the human race needed dragons. "Dragons," he concluded, "were necessary monsters." It is equally true that dragon-slayers are "necessary heroes." And the reasons for a civilization or even an individual choosing one monster or hero over another reveals a great deal about that culture or person. As one of the world's most popular heroes, there can be no doubt that King Arthur is a "necessary hero." Indeed, one might argue that he is almost the definitive hero of Western civilization. What is there about King Arthur that makes him so necessary for us? What does this say about him? What does it say about us? If we look at his origins and his progress through the centuries, we find that he is not just the "once and future king" but the eternal king who is a hero for all times and all cultures.

The motivation for reading and exploring the history, legend, myth and romance of King Arthur may be anything from idle curiosity to hard-core carbon-dated

Coming of Arthur – a Celtic knight's dream of the supreme warrior of his race, "the once and future king."

archaeology. In the end, however, there is no doubt that the more we learn about King Arthur in his many manifestations, the more we learn about ourselves – both collectively and individually.

If we wish to understand the phenomenon of King Arthur, we must begin at the beginning. We must examine the historical evidence left to us: the texts, chronicles, verses, myths, fragments of epic poems, inscriptions, symbols, graven images, graffiti. We must learn what we can of that heroic age of Arthur and the people who inhabited his long-vanished kingdom.

It must have seemed like the end of the world. The chroniclers tell us that the fifth century in Britain was a cataclysmic time of slaughter and "days as dark as nights." The Britons of that age were the Celtic people who are the ancestors of the modern Welsh. They had occupied the island for a thousand years. Since the first century, they had formed an integral part of the Roman Empire and their educated classes of clergy and aristocracy spoke Latin as well as Brythonic (an early form of Welsh). Consequently, although Britons were racially Celtic, they saw themselves as Romanized Christians who were bound economically, politically and culturally to an empire that was rapidly and disastrously collapsing.

The collapse had begun decades earlier, with the disaster of the Battle of Adrianople in 378, which marked the beginning of a massive invasion of barbarian horsemen from the East. At Adrianople, the Visigoth cavalry crushed the Roman Emperor Valens's legions of heavily armoured infantry. After Adrianople, horse-mounted warriors would dominate warfare in Europe for a thousand years. It was the dawn of the age of the horseman, the beginning of the apocalyptic age of "chivalry." It was also the beginning of the end of the Empire. Wave after wave of barbarian horsemen would batter down the monumental civilization of the Greco-Roman world. The Roman legions were trampled beneath the hooves of the Visigoths, Ostrogoths, Lombards, Franks, Slavs, Burgundians and Vandals. By 407, Rome had no choice but to withdraw the protection of her

Days as Dark as Nights – barbarian invaders swept across Europe. The Roman Empire was shattered, and Saxons, Picts and Scots pillaged Roman-Celtic Britain.

legions from Britain to fight invaders on the continent of Europe. (In 410 Rome herself was sacked by Alaric the Goth.) Britain was made independent and self-governing, but was soon embroiled in inter-tribal conflicts between various petty kingdoms. Without a single authority to organize a united defence, Britain was attacked by pagan barbarian invaders from the north, east and west. Christian Roman Britain was teetering on the edge of obliteration and was threatened with a headlong fall into an age of darkness.

To save themselves from being ruthlessly attacked by the pagan Picts and Irish, the Britons made a desperate alliance with the Angles of the Jutish chieftains Hengist and Horsa. The Angle mercenaries were given the southeast lands of Essex and part of Kent in exchange for driving the barbarian hordes back into the mountains north of the old Roman walls. For the Britons, no alliance could have been more disastrous. True to their word, the Angles played a decisive part in driving the Picts north beyond

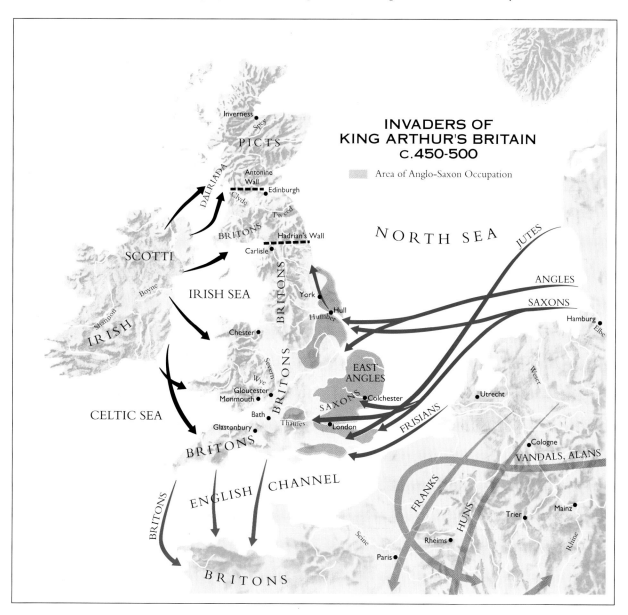

Hadrian's Wall, but they themselves eventually proved to be an even greater threat. Once given a safe foothold, Hengist and Horsa revolted against their hosts and paymasters. Soon, waves of Saxons, Angles, Jutes and Frisians arrived to reinforce the original mercenary army. Allied with the Picts, the northern attacks against the Britons as far south as York were renewed. As Angles and Saxons raided the whole of the east and southeast coast, they seized all of Kent, Essex, Sussex, East Anglia and Bernicia. Meanwhile, from northern Ireland the wild Gaelic pirates known as the "Scotti" (a Roman term meaning "bandit") launched random attacks along the length of the west coast and established the first Scots kingdom of Dalriada north-west of Loch Lomaine and the Antonine Wall. This series of disasters was deemed the fault of the British king Vortigern who had first extended the invitation to the Angles. The name Vortigern (meaning "overlord") was probably a title assumed by the most powerful clan chieftain of the Britons. In the end, Vortigern was attacked by both the Saxons and the Britons, who felt he had betrayed them, and came to a violent end.

The civilization of Roman-Celtic Britain – its forts, citadels, temples, churches, libraries and cities – was overrun, burned and obliterated as the barbarians swept all before them. Disaster followed disaster and the Britons were pushed back on every border. In the year 446, they sent one last plea for help to Roman Consul Aetius, the Military Commander of the Roman Forces of Gaul. There was no reply. The Empire was collapsing and Aetius had no time to consider the plight of the Britons. The Consul was desperately struggling to make an alliance with the Goths and Franks to create a single military force capable of withstanding the one terror they all feared: Attila the Hun.

There seemed no hope for the Britons. If ever a people needed a champion, it was the Britons of the late fifth century. Miraculously, not one, but two great champions united the Britons in a common cause and transformed their fortunes in war. The first champion was called Ambrosius Aurelianus; the second went by the name of Artorius.

According to Gildas, a British priest and scribe who wrote his *De Excidio Britorum* (*The Ruin of Britain*) in the early sixth century, "a remnant to whom miserable citizens gather from various lairs on all sides as keenly as a hive of bees under threat of storm...takes up arms and challenges the Saxons under Ambrosius Aurelianus." We are told Ambrosius Aurelianus was not really a Briton, but the "last of the Romans." There has been much speculation about Ambrosius Aurelianus, but archaeological evidence suggests that he was responsible for restoring trade with the Empire and re-establishing the rule of law and government. Certainly, imperial roads were repaired, while forts and walls were rebuilt and reoccupied during this time of renewed prosperity.

By what authority did Ambrosius Aurelianus take control? As a Roman aristocrat, he certainly was not considered a British king. The word "rex" or "king" was never used in association with Ambrosius Aurelianus, but he was frequently identified with the Roman government administrative titles of Comes Britanniarum

Opposite **Attila the Hun – so feared that Goths, Franks and Romans formed an alliance to fight him.** *Above* **Artorius – the Romanized Briton whose military genius was the salvation of his race.**

("Count of the Britons") or Dux Britannia ("Duke of Britain"). It is known that the emperor Honorius appointed a Roman aristocrat named Constantine as Britain's last senior governor or Comes Britanniarum just after 410. It has been suggested that Ambrosius Aurelianus was the son of Constantine, whose post was withdrawn in 418. After that time Britain became a self-governing state and the Britons reverted to the old Celtic system of tribal kings who rallied around the Vortigern. Perhaps the spectacular failure of Vortigern and the betrayal by the Angles resulted in an attempt to revive the old imperial government system which for nearly four centuries had unified the Britons. By whatever means he came to power, Ambrosius Aurelianus proved to be a capable governor and a competent organizer and commander, but he was not the warlord who left his mark on

the battlefields of history. That distinction belongs to his successor, a Romanized Briton named Artorius, a military leader of genius. Although Artorius did not assume the title Count of the Britons, he adopted the more aggressive Roman title of Dux Bellorum ("Duke" or "Lord of Battles"). We are told that Artorius – or Arthur, in its Brythonic form – the Dux Bellorum, led the Britons to victory in twelve mighty battles against the Saxon, Pict, Scot and Irish hordes. Time and again, the armoured British cavalry shattered the shield wall of the barbarian infantries and drove their armies from the field. The culmi-

nation was the Battle of Mons Badonicus (Badon Hill) where Arthur and his British cavalry were credited with slaughtering nine hundred Saxon warriors in a single final charge. This battle was a victory so bloody and complete that the Saxons sued for peace. For three decades after, it is claimed, the Saxons did not dare challenge the authority of the Britons. It was the brilliant warrior and architect of this truce with the Saxons, Arthur the Dux Bellorum, who provides the basis for the myths and legends of the com- posite character we now know as King Arthur.

The deeds of the Dux Bellorum were forever remembered by proud Britons. Arthur was not only the saviour of a people on the brink of extinction, but he gave them the glory of a dozen victories. The deeds of other heroes (including those of Arthur's mentor, Ambrosius Aurelianus) soon became associated with his name. With the Saxons pacified and the Picts and Irish subdued, the Britons were granted a time of peace and prosperity when their culture flowered once again. In tales and songs, this was the gold-

en era of the Britons when for the last time the whole nation came under the command of a single British leader. It was their heroic age and Arthur was their greatest hero. The ancient Welsh legends recorded in the *Mabinogion* speak of the ever-victorious Arthur, whose wrath was so great that when he drew his sword "flames of fire might be seen as from the

mouths of serpents, and so dreadful was he that none could look upon him." And so Arthur, Lord of Battles was gradually transformed into King Arthur – the very real symbol of the unconquerable spirit of the British race.

Opposite **Slaughter of the Saxons –
Artorius led the Britons in twelve
victorious battles in a decade.**
Above **King Arthur of the Thirty
Kingdoms – the transformation of a
historical warlord into a legendary
medieval emperor.**

CHAPTER TWO

ARTHUR DUX BELLORUM

The warrior Arthur, with the soldiers and kings of Britain…
was twelve times leader in war, and victor in all battles.
History of the Britons – *Nennius*

Artorius Dux Bellorum – the British Arthur, Lord of Battles – was the historical figure around whom the myths and legends of King Arthur whirled. But what do we really know of this man and of the people who followed him? Where was his long lost kingdom in that dark age? Can we know Arthur and his men by those deeds recorded in chronicles? Can we catch the gleam of his bright sword in an epic tale, or perceive a glint of light from his fierce eye in an ancient song or poem?

There are clues. From fragments of historical texts, we know something of the warlord's deeds and character. The warfare and turmoil of the Dark Age Saxon conquest left very little in the way of written records for nearly two centuries after Arthur's time. However, the oral tradition of the day was rich, and the stature of Arthur in the recitations of the bards would before long grow to god-like proportions among the Britons. History and myth would combine to make him the Alexander the Great of the British people.

As the commander of the elite British cavalry, Arthur the Dux Bellorum stood out at the head of his forces on a white horse. He was as renowned for his personal fearlessness as for his bold tactics in battle. The Dux Bellorum stood at the head of the army as was his right, with none before him but the enemy. He was flanked by two standard bearers holding aloft the image of the Golden Dragon on the right and a fluttering banner with the Red Dragon on the left. Arthur could not be mistaken for anyone other than the Lord of Battles. His cavalry helmet was mounted with a golden crest shaped like a dragon. He wore a golden torque around his neck and a burnished mail shirt and lightweight body armour of silver. In his belt was thrust a long dagger and from his tyrian blue sash hung the double-bladed Caliburn, the legendary sword forged in Avalon. Across his back Arthur slung his circular shield, the radiant Pridwen. Its bronze

Artorius, Lord of Battles – commander of the Celtic cavalry. The Dux Bellorum was the warlord of the North Kingdom of the Britons.

studs and boss were chased in gold and painted with the haloed image of the Virgin. In his right hand, Arthur held Rhon, his long-bladed Elf spear, and from its shaft fluttered a pennant bearing the image of a sword thrust into a stone. Behind Arthur came his cavalrymen, rank on rank, carrying shields marked with images both savage and sacred, with single- and triple-bladed spears. Some carried bows and javelins or long lances. Some wore iron helmets and wild animal skins. Others wore linen combined with plate armour or mail. Some wielded axes taken from the Saxons; still others proudly brandished their heavy Roman cavalry swords.

The secret of the historical Arthur's military success was his revival of the elite armoured Roman cavalry known as the "cataphracti" which had patrolled Britain during the third and fourth centuries. Arthur's adaptation of this highly mobile, highly disciplined cavalry against an enemy that was almost exclusively made up of infantry forces resulted in a military force that rapidly out-manoeuvred, out-flanked and outfought its more numerous foes. His twelve undisputed victories against the enemies of his people demonstrated Arthur's ability to command a force of armoured cavalrymen to devastating effect.

So who were these warrior people that Arthur led? Today all regions of Britain claim to be within Arthur's realm, although it is most widely believed that his battles and deeds were in the southwest of England. There is little doubt, however, that the historical Dux Bellorum, the saviour of Britain, lived and fought primarily in the most northern realm of the Britons, specifically in that continually embattled region between Hadrian's Wall and the Antonine Wall. This includes the Borders and Lake District of England and the Lowlands of Scotland, from the Firth of Forth to the southern bite of the Solway Firth.

In Arthur's time, this region was called the Gododdin (meaning "north"), the most northerly kingdom of the Britons. The Men of the North were made up of four great tribes, all said to be descended from the hero Coel, the legendary "Old King Cole" of the nursery rhymes. Arthur's tribe, the Votadini, were fiercely independent warriors who for four centuries had been in the front line against all comers in the Gododdin. Never conquered by anyone (before the Saxon invasion), the Men of the North had been allied with the Romans against the Picts and Scots. They usually commanded their own cavalry troops, but at other times, they served as troops within the Roman Legion's cavalry units. The people of the Gododdin were partially Romanized, semi-

Above **Hadrian's Wall – the inheritance of the Dux Bellorum for the defence of Britain.**
Opposite **Men of the North – the fierce warriors of the Gododdin in battle array.**

Christian Britons mixed with Picts and ruled by a dozen clan chieftains known as the "Twelve Kings of the North." It was among these people that Arthur rose to power and it was from their midst that the horsemen of his armies came. Voluntarily united in a common cause, as they had been during the great days of Rome, they were once again fighting under a single warlord, the Dux Bellorum. From his strategic location, Arthur had use of both Hadrian's Wall and the Antonine Wall with a total of thirty-six forts. He also controlled the massive fortification of the former Sixth Legion citadel of Carlisle on the south shore of the Solway Firth, on the western end of Hadrian's Wall. This was the primary military stronghold in the region. However, it is likely that the gathering place or governmental seat for the Kings of the North was further north, in the heartland of the Gododdin near Edinburgh, not far from the current royal seat of Holyrood and just below the mountain ridge that still carries the name Arthur's Seat.

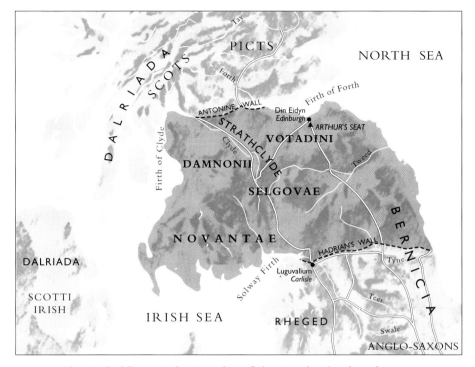

**The Gododdin – Arthur's realm of the North Kingdom between
Hadrian's Wall and the Antonine Wall, homeland of the four
tribes of Coel: the Votadini, Damnonii, Selgovae and Novantae.**

As the Romans clearly understood, the northern Border Country
was the most critical region for any military defence of Britain. Once
Hadrian's Wall was breached, nothing could stop barbarian armies from the
north, east and west. Through their strongly fortified passes, the Roman
roads of the North were the only routes invading Pict infantries could take
south. It was also the natural invasion route for the Irish from the west and
the Saxons from the east across the North Sea. Nor could the Irish or the
Saxons risk by-passing these borderlands by invading further south, because
they would soon find armies of Britons both before them and at their backs.

From the defenders' point of view, the Gododdin provided the best
defensive position in Britain. This was particularly true when the nation
was threatened by more than one enemy, because instead of stationing a
number of armies all along a defensive front, a single, large, fast-moving
cavalry might forcefully and rapidly respond to attacks on any side. There
was only a narrow neck of land between the North Sea and the Irish Sea
(that is, between the Firths of Clyde and Forth), so a single horse-mounted
army might easily cross from one coast to the other and respond to even the
most coordinated attacks.

Largely through the influence of the Roman clergy, many of the
Gododdin were fluent in Latin and were familiar with the history and literature of classical Greece and Rome. They may have been at the far edge of

the Empire but the imperial trade routes allowed them access to remarkable products from many parts of the world. Rich in both civilizations, their world was an exotic blend of Celtic and Roman art and culture.

This Dark Age of the historical Arthur was a time when the oral tradition of British bards and poets flourished. It was a time not unlike that of the Dark Age of Greece when Homer's epic poetry was composed and sung. The historical Arthur was almost an exact contemporary of the Anglo-Saxon Beowulf and the Burgundian heroes who inspired the epic tales of both the Norse *Volsunga Saga* and the German *Nibelungenlied*. Unfortunately, of all the epic tales of Arthur's time, none survives intact.

The great British bard of the time was Aneirin who is credited with the composition of the earliest Celtic epic. Called simply *The Gododdin*, it is the tale of a heroic last stand by Arthur's tribe, the Votadini Men of the North, and their extermination at the hands of the Saxons. Aneirin writes: "The Men of the North hastened forth, wearing torques, defending the land – and there was slaughter. Though they were slain they slew and they shall be honoured until the end of the world." By the eighth century, the Gododdin had been overrun and the Votadini Kingdom of the North was no more. Saxons, Picts and Scots scattered, subjugated and annihilated Arthur's people. Yet, so brave were they in their struggle against overwhelming forces that their deeds were preserved and – in spirit – passed on in the legend of their greatest leader, Arthur.

The Glens of the North Kingdom – the haunted battlegrounds of brutal Dark Age conflicts between the Men of the North and their many foes.

CHAPTER THREE

KINGDOM OF THE DRAGON

*Alas for the Red Dragon, for its end is near…Britain's mountains
and valleys shall be levelled, and its rivers shall run with blood.*
Prophecies of Merlin – *Geoffrey of Monmouth*

 In the world of myth and legend where King Arthur is still to be found, we are confronted with heraldic image and symbolic language more frequently than we are with straight historical fact. If we learn to read the images, they can provide us with a remarkable means of investigating the past. One of the most important heraldic images in the world of King Arthur was that of the dragon. There is something remarkable about the way in which the dragon appears in histories and texts in connection with Arthur. For example, on the occasion of Arthur's "glorious slaughter" of the Saxons at the Battle of Badon, the Dark Age Welsh bard Cynddelw sang a vivid battle song:

> The action of the Battle of Badon was shown
> in the day of the victorious dragon's anger;
> a track of shield-cleaving and shattering,
> a path with red blades…

Arthur is not – as one might have expected – a fairy tale dragon-slayer like England's Saint George. Quite the contrary, in this song the hero is himself the "victorious dragon" who slaughters the Saxons. The dragon is a manifestation of Arthur and his people. Today, everyone recognizes the image of the Red Dragon as emblematic of the Welsh people, the true descendants of the ancient Britons. The Welsh, or the Cymry, as they prefer to be known ("Welsh" being Anglo-Saxon for "slave"), are the People of the Red Dragon and this beast is the central feature of their national flag. But where did the Welsh acquire their dragon, and when and how did the Red Dragon, Arthur the Dux Bellorum and the Britons come together?

In fact, the few texts that have survived contain two legends about dragons. The first of these tales relates exactly how the Britons acquired the Red Dragon as their heraldic beast. The second legend provides the link between the Dragon and Arthur the Dux Bellorum. The story of "The Red and the White Dragon" is set in the time of Vortigern,

the "overlord" or High King of the Britons, during the mid-fifth-century revolt of the Anglo-Saxons of Hengist and Horsa. It has frequently been interpreted as a parable about the fall of a king who builds on the shifting sands of dubious morality and false belief. In fact, though, its main purpose is to present and explain the heraldic animal of the Britons. Curiously, this legend not only serves to link the Britons to their heraldic animal, but is also the story of the origin of the greatest prophet and most important spiritual guide of that race, Merlin the Magician.

The Victorious Dragon – a knight displays the heraldic dragon of Britain's ancient kings. The dragon was emblematic of Arthur's people and their heirs, the people of Wales.

THE RED AND THE
WHITE DRAGON

When he saw the devastation of the British people whom he had betrayed, the High King Vortigern did not try to turn back the Saxon invaders. Instead, he commanded his magicians to tell him how he might best secure his own life. They advised him to build a strong tower high in the mountains, so that if all other fortresses should fall he might find safety there. Soon masons assembled by the cowardly Vortigern began to lay the foundations of the tower, but however much they built by day, the earth swallowed their work up by night. Some terrible enchantment was cast upon this place, so again Vortigern called his magicians. They told him that a sacrifice must be made or the foundations would never remain. Vortigern's soldiers must find a child without an earthly father. That child must be sacrificed, his blood mixed with the mortar and then sprinkled on the stones. Only then would the foundations become sound and the great tower raised. It happened that there was just such a child. Born of a princess who was a virgin nun, the child's father was an incubus demon from the region of the night that lay between the moon and the earth. These demons were in part men and in part angels, but unholy. In fact, this child might have been an anti-Christ, had it not been for the wisdom and piety of his mother, who had the child baptized at the moment of birth, so driving out evil but keeping his supernatural nature.

When the demon-child was brought before Vortigern, the King saw great authority in the youngster's bearing. Learning what his fate might be, the child challenged the authority of the magicians and claimed that he alone knew the reason why the foundations of the tower would not hold firm. "You who have ordered my blood to be scattered on the stones, tell me now what lies hidden under the foundation? For there is the thing that prevents the walls from holding firm." To this the magicians were silent and the child mocked them and told the King that if he summoned his workmen and ordered them to dig, they would soon find a deep pool beneath the foundation that was the cause of the shifting earth beneath the foundation stones.

When the King ordered his workmen to do as the child commanded, he indeed found the deep pool that had been prophesied. Again the child mocked the magicians. "Tell me now, you wise men, what lies beneath the pool?" Again the magicians were silent before the demon-child's fierce gaze. The child then turned to Vortigern and said, "Command your workmen to drain the pool and at the bottom there will you find two huge hollow stones that roll and slide about in the watery pit. Inside those stones you will see two mighty dragons who are sleeping." The King was amazed at the child's prediction, but he did not doubt his eyes when the pool was drained and two hollow stones were found in the ebbing waters of the lake. Yet, still Vortigern and all the assembled workmen and soldiers and magicians gave up a great cry when the two hollow stones burst with a mighty blast and

there appeared two huge dragons, one white and one red. But from them the men had nothing to fear, for the dragons had eyes only for one another. They leapt to fiercely attack each other, panting fire and tearing away at flesh with talons and teeth.

When Vortigern asked what this battle meant, the demon-child burst into tears and sank into a trance, replying in a strange voice, "O my lord, weep for the Red Dragon for his end is near. His dwelling place shall soon be occupied by the White Dragon, who is the Saxons you have welcomed into your kingdom. The Red Dragon is the people of Britain, who will be driven out by the brood of the White Dragon. The valleys of Britain shall be emptied, the mountains shall be stripped and the rivers shall run with blood. Cities shall be pillaged, churches burned and the people slain or oppressed. Calamity shall come to all you have known in your kingdom."

Vortigern grew fearful when he heard this account, yet he believed the words of the demon-child. He then asked by what name the child was known and offered him a great reward if he might give the King some hopeful prophecy to save his life in the disasters ahead. It was then the demon child told Vortigern that his name was Emrys Merlin. He could accept no reward for his prophecies because they brought no comfort: the young Merlin foresaw Vortigern in a tall tower set afire. Terrified by this prophecy, Vortigern fled, but it did him no good. The armies of the betrayed Britons found him anyway. He could not escape his fate, for in retreat he climbed the tower of a vassal which was set ablaze and just as Merlin the demon child had prophesied, Vortigern was consumed by flames.

Opposite **Birth of Merlin – the supernatural and prophetic child of a virgin nun and a demon.**
Above **Battle of the Dragons – revealed by the prophecies of Merlin.**

The second legend was that of "The Dragon Star." This is a tableau in which Merlin the Magician presents proof of the celestial approval of Uther Pendragon – and his son Arthur after him – as the king of the Britons after the murder of Ambrosius Aurelius (Aurelianus). The appearance of the hero is foreshadowed like that of Christ by a bright star, which in this case is obviously a twin-tailed comet.

The account is taken from *The History of the Kings of Britain* written in the twelfth century, but the incident comes from an earlier source. This version mistakenly identifies Aurelius and Uther as brothers who along with Arthur are said to be kings of Britain. But they were not kings: Aurelius was a Roman Comes Britanniarum while Uther and Arthur were both Britons who took the post of the Dux Bellorum. The purpose of the original story was to establish the connection between the Roman Dux Bellorum and the Briton Pendragon. Once again it is Merlin who interprets events. He is now the resident royal magician and prophet of the Britons who establishes royal pedigrees and certifies tribal titles by interpreting supernatural signs.

THE DRAGON STAR

On the eve of the treacherous murder of King Ambrosius Aurelius of the Britons, all the people of the island were struck with fear and amazement when a star of great magnitude and brilliance appeared in the sky. The star was like a great ball of fire spread out in the shape of a dragon. From the fiery dragon's head extended two tails of light. One was straight and bright from the south and Gaul; the other split up into seven smaller shafts of light from the west and the Irish Sea.

Uther, the King's brother, was leading the British army in a campaign against the Saxons when the star appeared, and news of his brother's death had not yet reached him. So he called for the royal magician Merlin in order that the wise man might tell him the meaning of the fiery Dragon Star in the sky.

Merlin burst into tears and fell into an oracular trance. Then, summoning his prophetic voice, the Magician spoke. "Lord, our loss is beyond repair! The Britons are orphaned. The divine Ambrosius Aurelius, our 'greatest king, has perished. His death is our death, unless the army of the British Dragon is victorious against the Saxons. Strike now, Uther. Victory shall be yours and you shall be king of all Britons in your brother's place. The fiery Dragon Star signifies Uther in person and one tail of light signifies your son, who will be a great man. He will rule as king after you and his dominion will extend over all of Gaul as well as Britain. The second ray signifies your daughter, whose sons and grandsons shall one after the other rule as the seven kings of the Britons."

Soon after this the Britons indeed met the Saxons in battle and Uther's army was victorious. Only then did Uther finally learn that his brother Ambrosius Aurelius had in fact died, just as Merlin had predicted. Full of sadness at this news, but flushed with his triumphant victory, Uther was crowned the new king of the Britons. To mark the occasion of Merlin's prophecy of the Dragon Star, Uther had two dragons fashioned out of gold. They were very like the fiery dragon he had seen in the sky, and were marvellously crafted creatures. One was sent to the cathedral where it presided over the archbishop's congregation at prayer, while the other Uther kept for himself as a standard that he carried with him into battle. From that time onwards Uther became known as Uther Pendragon, which in the British language meant the "dragon's head."

In these two tales, the Britons are formally being presented with their national heraldic beast. It is clear from these stories that the symbol of the dragon was at that time unknown to the Britons. After all, if everyone already knew the meaning of the two dragons, why would they need a supernatural child such as Merlin to interpret their fierce battle? Before that incident, the Britons had never identified with the Red Dragon, just as the title "Pendragon" had never before been used for the leader of their army. Historically, there is no doubt that the title Pendragon was used as a specific reference to the Dux Bellorum, the Roman title the historical Arthur adopted as the overall head of the British military. Furthermore, the image of the Red Dragon was emblazoned on British flags and banners and accepted by friends and foes alike as symbolic of the British people during Arthur's time and forever after.

St George the Dragon-Slayer – such Anglo-Saxon heroes were slayers of dragons, the heraldic animals of their foes, the Celtic Britons.

Although the Celtic heroes sometimes smite a few serpents here and there, they are not generally noted as dragon-slayers. That seems to be left to their enemies, Germanic heroes such as Siegfried, Sigurd, Beowulf and even the English Saint George. The plethora of Saxon and Viking tales about dragon-slaying heroes driving legions of dragons from the monster-haunted British Isles, show a mythic version of the historic retreat of the Britons: the Red Dragon People grudgingly withdrawing into the most remote and mountainous parts of the nation. In the myths of the Saxon conquerors, the land of Britain was being cleared of the dragon race.

Even so, for a time after Arthur's death in the first part of the sixth century, the Kingdom of the Red Dragon remained the wealthiest, most civilized and most powerful on the island. It took over a century for that to change. In 700, the Britons were an independent people occupying Wales, the Strathclyde, Cornwall and Brittany, and it was not until 926 that Cornwall was forced to accept Anglo-Saxon rule and the Britons were contained like brooding dragons within the mountains of Wales. In 927 the Anglo-Saxons united "England" for the first time under one leader when Athelstan became the first king of England. The dominion of the Saxon kings was soon broken by the Danish King Canute and although the Saxon kings regained the throne after the Danes, they did not keep it for long. In 1066, William the Conqueror invaded with his Norman knights and seized the crown with his mailed fist.

Curiously, when William and his heirs were casting about for some means of defending their right to rule Britain, they put forward a claim that must have baffled the Britons: despite the fact that he was a Norman, it was argued that William was actually the true heir of King Arthur! By virtue of Norman intermarriage with the Bretons of Brittany, William the Conqueror claimed descent from King Arthur through his Breton blood – and so laid claim to the Red Dragon standard. Only one thing made William the Conqueror's

Lair of the Dragons – the caverns of Mount Snowden in northern Wales where, according to some legends, lie Arthur's knights. Like sleeping dragons, the immortal warriors await the call to do battle with the foes of their nation.

c.500 *c.700* *c.850* *c.1000*

claim as the heir to the Kingdom of the Dragon at all believable: when William of Normandy launched his invasion of Britain, by astonishingly good luck a great comet appeared in the heavens above Britain. It was so bright, it could be seen by day and by night and it caused much fear and wonder among the Britons. Was this the Dragon Star, the certain sign of divine approval for the return of the heirs of Arthur to the British throne? William seized this opportunity and sent word ahead to the Saxons that while the Dragon Star blazed in the heavens he would fulfil the ancient prophecy of a new Arthur, laying low the Saxon interlopers and seizing Arthur's crown. He was a man of his word. The action of the Battle of Hastings "was shown in the day of the victorious dragon's anger; a track of shield-cleaving and shattering, a path of red blades."

Above **Retreat of the Red Dragon people to the mountains of Wales.** *Below* **Alfred, Arthur and Canute – three bloodlines of Britain: Anglo-Saxon, Celt and Scandinavian, manifest in the images of her kings.**

CHAPTER FOUR

THE SWORD IN THE STONE

Whosoever pull this sword out of this anvil and stone
is the rightful king of all England.
Le Morte d'Arthur - *Malory*

 Just as the Red Dragon can be used as a guide to the Arthurian world, other emblematic devices shed light into the deep recesses of the Dark Ages. One of the most famous episodes in Arthurian Romance is the story of an unknown youth who proves his right to be king by miraculously pulling a sword from a stone. The Sword in the Stone and King Arthur have become inseparable in the popular mind. But where does the vivid image and its legend come from? Is it a motif that originates with Arthur or does it have its antecedents in an even more remote tradition? Can we find, as we did with the Red Dragon, any link between the Sword in the Stone and the historical Arthur? Let us begin with the story itself, which derives from Malory.

THE ORACLE OF THE SWORD

After the death of the king of the Britons, Uther Pendragon, there was great strife throughout the land because there was no clear successor, and no single baron was powerful enough to subjugate the others. With all this internal conflict, the realm was left open to invasion and slaughter by foreign barbarians. So Merlin sent word that all the barons and knights of the land must gather in one place to hold a tournament and there decide who might take the crown and rule the kingdom. They all came, not for love of the magician, but for fear of his power. Also, he had been chief adviser to Uther Pendragon and knew the King's wishes on the night he breathed his last. But when the noblemen gathered for the tournament, they found that Merlin had not come. Instead, they saw a huge stone with a naked sword of the brightest steel plunged deep into it. And in the blade of the sword were inscribed letters of gold, "Whoever pulls this sword from the stone is the rightful king of Britain." Each knight and baron who had reason to claim the throne attempted to pull the sword from the stone. One by one they all failed. So, the tournaments were held open to all

who might come and try their strength. Having won at the joust, a champion might try his skill at drawing the sword from the stone. Among those who came was Sir Ector, once a loyal liegeman to Uther. He brought his young son, Sir Kay, who had just been given the honour of knighthood and was preparing to compete in the jousts.

On the day of his joust, when Sir Kay arrived at the tournament he realized that he had forgotten his sword at his lodgings. Much disturbed, he asked his young brother to go back for it. The young lad was glad to serve his brother, but though he rode to fetch the sword, he could not find it. He despaired, but as he returned to the tournament grounds he saw a strange thing: a sword thrust into a stone. Knowing nothing of the sword, the boy effortlessly pulled the blade from the stone and took it to his brother. When Sir Kay saw the shining blade, he recognized it at once and he took it to Ector, saying

"Here father is the sword from the stone. Does this mean I am the king of this land?"

Arthur Draws the Sword from the Stone – and demonstrates his right to be king of the Britons.

31

But Sir Ector was a wise and honest man who knew the danger of taking things at face value. He asked his son who had given the sword to him and Kay confessed that it had been Arthur who had drawn the blade from the stone. Sir Ector did not doubt what he heard and he went at once to his youngest son, fell upon his knee and swore his loyalty to the new king of the Britons. Then Sir Ector told Arthur that he was not his real father. Arthur was in truth the son of a high-born noble. As a baby his life had been endangered and so Merlin the Magician had delivered him to Ector to be raised in secret as Ector's son. When the knights and barons of the land learned that a fifteen-year-old boy had been selected as their new king, there was a gasp of disbelief as well as much discord. Patiently Arthur sheathed the sword again in the stone and allowed all who wished to try their strength. But still, they all failed. Only the boy could draw it out and he did so without effort. Finally all agreed that the oracle of the Sword in the Stone had spoken and the boy named Arthur was the chosen one: the true king of the Britons.

The drawing of a sword from a stone is a metaphor for the science of metallurgy, itself a drawing-out of iron from ore or stone. (The metallurgical cult aspect or image of the Sword in the Stone is made even more plain in several versions of Arthur's tale where the sword is actually in an anvil sitting on a stone.) In earlier times the secrets of metallurgy were the equivalent of today's atomic secrets. A nation that acquired the secret of smelting iron and forging metal was able to obliterate its less technologically advanced neighbour. And as the science of metallurgy advanced throughout the Iron Age, a new innovation (forging superior steel, or making armour or chain mail) would result in a chain reaction of revolutions, mass migrations, murderous conquests and collapsing empires.

The secrets of metallurgy were controlled by alchemists and smiths. Protective of their craft, these men often lived in closed societies with little contact with the rest of the culture and they were frequently hidden deep in mountain or forest refuges where enemies could not find them. Surrounded by mystery and isolated from the rest of the population, an aura grew around these metallurgical specialists and they were perceived to have a special kind of power over even the

Dwarf Smith – in many Celtic, Germanic and Norse legends supernatural weapons were forged by these powerful metal-workers.

mightiest nobles of the kingdom. Consequently, these outcast alchemists
and smiths acquired an ambivalent reputation. They were both feared and
respected by the general population and over time they were also mytholo-
gized, emerging as the supernatural wizards and dwarfs of Norse, German
and Celtic myths and legends.

Kings and knights obviously put a high value on these metal-making
wizards and dwarfs. They fiercely guarded their own while trying to kidnap
or kill the "evil" wizards and dwarfs of neighbouring kingdoms. Wizards
and dwarfs who attempted to set up their own kingdoms were portrayed as
satanic monsters because they not only threatened individual monarchs, but
endangered the whole social order. If a man could rule on the basis of his
skills rather than by a divinely ordained birthright, then the monopoly of
power held by the aristocratic classes would soon deteriorate. Thus each
ruler strove to maintain a careful balance wherein his metallurgists were
content yet firmly under control, but this was not always possible. Merlin is
one example of a wizard who held the real key to power in a kingdom. In
the story of the Sword in the Stone, it is Merlin the Wizard who controls
the succession to the crown. But by drawing the sword from the stone,
Arthur symbolically demonstrates that he is supported by – and has power
over – the supernatural beings capable of provid-
ing the whole society with the weapons and tools
that were its lifeblood.

**Alchemists – feared and revered in
equal measure: metallurgy became
the primary factor in the dominion
of one nation over another.**

Variations on the Sword in the Stone motif as a vehicle for dynastic succession are emphatically displayed in Germanic legends, but most fully in the Norse *Volsunga Saga*. In this greatest of all Viking sagas can be found the model for Arthur's Sword in the Stone. The tale also provides some clues to the origin of Merlin the Magician, who can clearly be seen in the character of Odin, the Vikings' all powerful wizard-god.

THE SWORD OF THE VOLSUNGS

The dynastic House of King Volsung was raised around a huge sacred tree called Branstock and as this tree was the central pillar of the structure, the great hall itself came to be known by this name. No traveller was turned away from Branstock and one night late, there came an old, one-eyed visitor, seeking shelter from a bitter storm. Although many of the assembled guests did not care for the wily appearance of the silent old man, Volsung, with due respect for his age, treated him courteously and well. After a time, when the traveller had eaten and drunk his fill, he stood up, opened his cape and revealed a marvellous glittering sword. The guests drew back in alarm, but the old man turned from them and, with supernatural strength, thrust the blade hilt-deep into the great tree.

His single wizard's eye glinting, the old man declared to the King and his guests that this weapon was to be the gift of the gods to the warrior who could draw it from its wooden sheath. He then walked out of the hall and vanished into the night. None doubted that the old man who had visited them was Odin the All-Father, the one-eyed king of the gods, known to travel the world in the guise of an old wizard and work many feats of wonder. The god-given sword was the dream of every great warrior, so all the men of the hall vied for a chance to win it. But none could draw it from the tree, including nine of Volsung's ten sons, all of them strong and brave men. Finally, however, Volsung's youngest son Sigmund placed his hand on the hilt and used all his tremendous strength. To his total amazement the sword eased out of the tree and became his prize. Sigmund the Volsung was Odin's chosen champion. With that great blade that could slice through stone and steel, Sigmund and his son Sigurd were to win fame greater than any mortal before them. By the sword's power, armies were defeated, kings were overthrown, giants were slain and a terrible dragon was slaughtered.

The Sword of the Volsungs – driven into the Branstock tree by Odin, the great god of wizards.

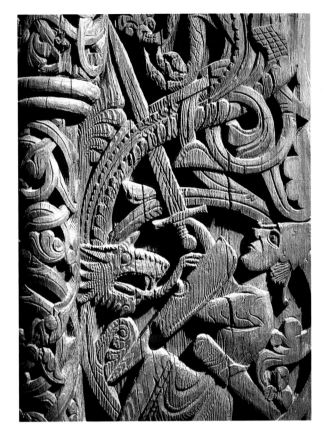

Both "The Sword in the Stone" and "The Sword of the Volsungs" demonstrate how a true hero and heir needs none of the trappings of royalty to prove his worth. Real nobility of spirit cannot be denied, though it may walk about the world in disguise. It is clear that Arthur's stone-drawn sword bestowed upon him some of the heroic prestige found in the earlier Norse tale. But the drawing of the sword from the stone is not just another of the myriad attributes of Arthur, it is perhaps the hero's most defining moment. Is there thus another precedent for the Sword in the Stone motif that can explain why it is so deeply etched in Arthurian legend?

In fact a connection has surfaced that links the fifth-century Arthur and the Sword in the Stone motif, and not surprisingly it was proposed by an expert in heraldry, the American historian Dr Helmet Nickel. Dr Nickel has studied heraldic or emblematic links between the historical Arthur and both the Red Dragon and the Sword in the Stone. The origins of both emblems confirm the identity of Arthur as commander of a revived Roman cavalry. We know from Roman military records that this was the elite regiment of the Roman Sixth Legion which manned Hadrian's Wall for more than two centuries. The Legion's cavalry during the Roman occupation was largely made up of Sarmatians, a remarkable race of horsemen from the plains north of the Black Sea. They are portrayed in relief sculptures in Chester and graffiti drawings near Hadrian's Wall. During the

Sigurd the Dragon-slayer – with the ancestral sword of the Volsungs, the hero slays the dragon and wins his birthright.

third and fourth centuries over 15,000 Sarmatians were stationed in Britain and many settled there and intermarried with Britons of the Gododdin.

The Sarmatians were the first to utilize two technological advances, the stirrup and chain mail. Consequently, they created the first heavy armoured cavalry in Europe. Chain mail had obvious advantages, but the stirrup was the more important innovation. Before the stirrup any cavalry-man attempting to lance a foot soldier usually slid off his horse. After the stirrup was introduced the role of cavalry changed from a harassment force into a full scale assault force. The Sarmatian heavy cavalry was the most advanced and dangerous fighting force in Europe, although the Roman commanders who hired them as mercenaries continued to use them in the traditional cavalry roles of patrolling and harassing. However, had the Romans adopted Sarmatian technology on a large scale, the history of the world would have been radically different.

As portrayed in the carvings and graffiti drawings, the Sixth Legion carried into battle two standards. One was a red dragon. The second was an emblem unique to the Sarmatian cavalry: an image of a naked sword thrust into a stone! It appears to be a Sarmatian tribal icon or religious

symbol that soon became the Sarmatian Cavalry insignia. It is very likely that Arthur's cavalry (many undoubtedly of mixed Sarmatian-Votadini blood) retained that insignia with the same sort of pride that many soldiers have today for their own regimental insignias – sewn on clothing, marked in jewellery and even tattooed on their arms.

Is this the reason why the Sword in the Stone motif is so deeply embedded in Arthurian legends? Does the legend amount to a "just so story" explaining a regimental and racial icon of Arthur's heroic cavalrymen? We may never know the answer to this question. But the story of "The Sword in the Stone" provides us with a classic case of how legends and historical truth accrete like the layers of a pearl until they form a perfect glistening whole. The primary association of the historical Arthur with the Sarmatian symbol of a sword in a stone is overlaid with the hallowed Norse story of "The Sword of the Volsungs." Finally, the techno-political metaphor of metallurgy is applied, and the result is the story of "The Sword in the Stone," one of the most resonant images in the entire Arthurian canon.

Sarmatian Cavalryman – a Roman graffiti drawing of one of the Asiatic horsemen of the Sixth Legion, complete with full mail armour.

MAGNUS ARTURUS REX

CHAPTER FIVE

ARTHUR THE KING

*So was Arthur sworn to be true king, to stand with true justice
from thenceforth for all the days of his life.*
Le Morte d'Arthur - *Malory*

How does one explain the elevation of the obscure Arthur Dux Bellorum to one of the most colossal heroes in the literature and popular culture of the English-speaking world? Although it depends in part on the skill and imagination of story-tellers and poets, the dominance of Arthurian Romance in the Middle Ages had much more to do with the political and social realities of a particular medieval society than it did with its merit as literature. The truth is, much of King Arthur's story was manipulated to suit the political needs of the time in which it was written. To understand how and why, it is necessary to examine the earliest written accounts of King Arthur.

The adventures of King Arthur had been spread by minstrels and bards through much of Europe by the ninth century. However, it wasn't until the twelfth century that an extensive account of Arthur's life was written down. The first "life and times" of King Arthur was written in 1135, the last year of the reign of the Norman King Henry I. The story of Arthur was the focus of a book called the *Historia Regum Britanniae*, or *The History of the Kings of Britain*. The author was a Norman-Breton cleric who became known as Geoffrey of Monmouth. He claimed his book was a true history of all Britain's kings. In fact, it is a bizarre combination of fact and fiction that has and will forever inspire, baffle and enrage its readers.

Reading it today, *The History of the Kings of Britain* appears to be a quaint (and occasionally comic) work of fiction: for example, what historical source did Geoffrey of Monmouth have for the bizarre invasion of Britain by the 160,000-strong army of Africa's King Gormund? So it comes as something of a surprise to learn that *The History of the Kings of Britain* has proved to be one of the most influential books in the whole of European history. Its contents have been used to justify wars that have resulted in the slaughter of millions of people and its account of King Arthur's life has been manipulated by almost every British sovereign to

King Arthur – the legend of the fifth-century warlord changed over the centuries: the early medieval period saw his promotion from warlord to feudal king.

prove his or her right to rule. Furthermore, it was used as the factual and legal basis for five centuries of war between France and Britain.

Although it was badly "reviewed" by the scholars of its own time, Geoffrey of Monmouth's *History of the Kings of Britain* certainly pleased someone: the ruling Norman aristocracy, and particularly, the heirs of William the Conqueror. Indeed, we find that Geoffrey's version of King Arthur is clearly politically motivated by his desire – as the historian J.S.B. Tatlock once suggested – to give "a precedent for the dominions and ambitions of the Norman kings." To achieve this end, Geoffrey of Monmouth

The Four Norman Kings – William I, Wiliam Rufus, Henry I and Stephen. These French dukes justified their quasi-legal right to the British crown by claiming descent from Arthur.

was willing to turn history on its head. We are told that the Roman Occupation of Britain never happened and that British kings conquered Rome no less than three times. Furthermore, we find King Arthur transformed from Rome's last champion to Rome's most feared opponent! The motive behind this "historical inflation" was the bitter twelfth-century political and ecclesiastical conflicts between the Norman kings and the pope in Rome.

To be fair, Geoffrey of Monmouth was rewriting history no more than did the ancient Roman poet Virgil in his epic *Aeneid* or the Latin historian Livy in his *Early History of Rome*. Geoffrey of Monmouth created noble ancestors for the British in the same way that Virgil and Livy had created the heroes Aeneas and Romulus from fragments of myth and history in order to invent a pedigree for the Romans. The problem was that *The History of the Kings of Britain* was frequently used as a "true history," and whatever its artistic merits, the "true history" of King Arthur (and its various versions by other authors) became a highly charged political issue in the twelfth century and remained so for another five centuries. It is an ambitious work, covering a period of over 1,800 years. From the time of Britain's founding in 1115 BC until the exile of the last king of the Britons in AD 689, Geoffrey of Monmouth chronicles the lives and deeds of ninety-nine kings of Britain, although the bulk of the book is concerned with the lives of only a dozen of these kings. The history is told in five parts: "The Founding of Britain," "Britons and Romans," "The House of Constantine," "The Life of Arthur" and "Exile."

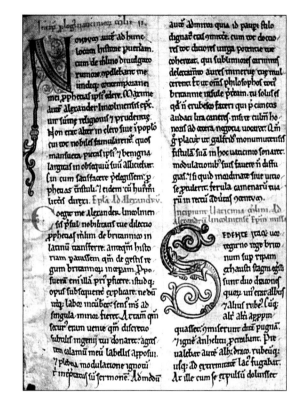

THE HISTORY OF THE KINGS OF BRITAIN

I. THE FOUNDING OF BRITAIN The best of all islands in the Western Ocean was Britain, a land of five races Normans, Britons, Saxons, Picts and Scots founded by Brutus, a descendant of Prince Aeneas of Troy. Brutus's three sons divided Britain into three parts, England, Wales and Scotland. A later descendant, Belinus, built the straight stone roads that cross Britain north-to-south and east-to-west. Together with his brother Brennius (the ruler of Normandy with whom he had previously had a dispute), Belinus made war on the Franks, the Germans and the Italians. The brothers then sacked Rome and became masters of Europe.

This account of the Britons' racial origin was obviously modelled on Virgil's *Aeneid* in which Aeneas fled Troy to found Rome. Geoffrey's point was that both the Britons and the Romans were descended from royal Trojans and were, therefore, of equal status. Geoffrey was careful to set mythical events solidly and specifically in the real geography of Britain, and fictional heroes were given authority through their interaction with famous historical figures. Imaginary events occurred at precise dates in the context of the history of Greece, Rome and the Holy Land.

Not wishing to acknowledge Roman superiority in any area, Geoffrey attributes the construction of all the straight Roman roads and massive stone temples and civic buildings to British kings. The British are also attributed with the conquest of the Roman Empire in 390 BC,

Historia Regum Britanniae – **Geoffrey of Monmouth's twelfth-century "history" was the basis of nearly all subsequent Arthurian literature.**

long before the Romans appeared on Britain's shores. As for Geoffrey's invention of the dispute and resolution between King Belinus of Britain and his brother King Brennius of Normandy, it was planted in the *History* for two reasons. The first is that it mirrored the conflict between William the Conqueror's two sons – one ruling in Britain, the other in Normandy. Secondly, and more importantly, it established an ancient precedent for the Norman-Breton alliance and suggested their predestination as the natural inheritors of the Roman Empire.

II. BRITONS AND ROMANS No less a personage than Julius Caesar recognized that both the Romans and the Britons were descended from Aeneas. Although the Britons agreed to pay tribute to Caesar, they were never conquered or occupied by the Romans. Rome's influence gradually increased until the time of Constantine, who led the Britons across the continent and conquered Rome, thereby becoming Constantine the Great. The next great king of Britain, Maximianus, conquered Armorica, where he founded a Second Britain, or Brittany. He then became the third British king to conquer Rome. However, when Maximianus was murdered the British soldiers were scattered across the various parts of the Empire and the British peasants were thus left abandoned and defenceless. Having no one else to turn to, the peasantry in desperation sent envoys to Rome, offering up their liberty in return for Roman protection from the barbarians. Rome acceded and sent its legions to Britain.

Trojan Ancestors – in Geoffrey's *History* Britain was founded by the Trojan prince Brutus, a legend imitative of Virgil's invention of the Roman progenitor, Aeneas.

42

Geoffrey of Monmouth's aim was to present history in such a way as to remove any Roman claim of sovereignty over Britain through historical precedent. He was also keen to praise the extraordinary military prowess of the Britons who, like Arthur, could never lose a battle (but somehow tended to lose the wars – usually because of internal conflicts) with the implied threat that the twelfth-century Norman-Breton rulers might revolt against Rome. This veiled threat of Norman-Bretons marching on Rome was not a hollow boast. Norman relatives of William the Conqueror who ruled Sicily had already sacked Rome once in the eleventh century and would actually do so twice more in the next century. Geoffrey of Monmouth's legendary founding of Armorica (Brittany) is introduced to further boost the importance of the Bretons. The deterioration of the Welsh Britons is explained by the loss of their aristocracy and warrior-caste, which either migrated to Armorica or was destroyed on the continent by the Romans. The noble Armorica Britons were thus the only ones left who would later be able to defend their ravaged kin in Britain against the Saxon invasions.

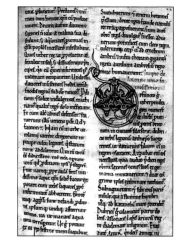

III. THE HOUSE OF CONSTANTINE

In the fifth century the Romans withdrew for the last time, leaving Britain to the Picts, Scots, Norwegians and Danes. The Britons were in desperate straits until the arrival from Armorica of Constantine II, the founder of the House of Constantine and father of three sons: Constans, Aurelius Ambrosius and Uther – who later was called Pendragon. Together

they drove the barbarians from the island and there was a decade of peace until Constantine was assassinated by Vortigern, who seized the throne. Terrified of the Picts, he made an alliance with the warlords of the Jutish chieftains, Hengist and Horsa, and allowed them to occupy Kent and Northumbria, but the Saxons later joined forces with the Picts and the plight of the Britons was worse than ever. Finally, Vortigern committed the ultimate betrayal of his own people. He called a council of peace at Salisbury with 460 of the greatest earls of the Britons. But he had tipped off the Saxons and they came armed with daggers hidden in their boots to murder all the Britons. It was after this disaster that Vortigern tried to build his tower and there came the prophetic child called Merlin who revealed the miracle of the Red and White Dragons and prophesied the fiery death of Vortigern and the pacification of the Saxons and Picts by the Armorica Britons led by Aurelius Ambrosius. And in fact peace did come with the crowning of King

Left Vortigern's Tower – the death of the tyrant in a tower of flames. *Above* Part fact, part invention – Geoffrey's work was reproduced many times over the centuries.

Aurelius, as did the restoration of the cities, roads and monasteries. Merlin and Uther went on a quest to Ireland and returned with the monument called the Giants' Ring (Stonehenge) which was miraculously erected over the site of the murdered earls on Salisbury Plain. Anarchy returned when King Aurelius was poisoned. By the appearance of a Dragon-Star (comet) in the sky, Merlin understood that Aurelius was dead, but saw that God willed Uther to be king and would carry the name Pendragon. Valiant Uther Pendragon soon conquered his enemies; and through Merlin's enchantments he won the beautiful Igraine (Ygerna), the wife of the Duke of Cornwall. Their child was conceived in secret and was raised to be the true heir of the Pendragon.

Geoffrey of Monmouth's agenda was to firmly establish the Saxons as an inferior and treacherous race that must be controlled. The Breton-Norman ruling warrior class of his day made up only about five percent of the population and thus both the Welsh and the Normans had a common cause in the suppression of the Saxons who made up the majority. This part of the book also established the pedigree of the future King Arthur. Merlin the Magician was the critical figure here. He presided over the courts of the British kings and directed the events of history. He also presided over Arthur's conception and was the witness for his legitimacy. This episode appears to have been written specifically in order to link the circumstances of Arthur's birth with the questionable

Merlin the Prophet – the legend of a prophetic child and druidic priest merged in Merlin the Wizard of the Pendragon Dynasty.

origins of William the Conquerer (who was also known as William the Bastard), or even with those of Geoffrey's immediate patron Robert of Gloucester (to whom he dedicated his *History of the Kings of Britain*), the illegitimate son of Henry I. However, the most obvious rigging of history to fit the politics of Norman Britain was the appearance of the "miraculous" comet that foretold the coming of Uther Pendragon and Arthur. The appearance of the comet in the sky when William the Conqueror invaded Britain was famous in Geoffrey's time. The Pendragon comet appears to be an episode that Geoffrey of Monmouth invented to link William with Uther Pendragon and Arthur.

IV. THE LIFE OF ARTHUR When Uther Pendragon lay in his tomb beneath the Giants' Ring, his fifteen-year-old son was crowned at Caerleon-on-Usk. King Arthur had no equal as an open-handed lord and an iron-fisted warrior. One victory followed another as Arthur made war on the Saxons, Scots and Picts. Twelve battles were fought and won by Arthur, whose warrior spirit shone as bright as his sword, the Avalon-forged Caliburn. After the last battle at Bath, all Britain (including Scotland and Wales) was pacified and all enemies were driven from its shores.

Soon after he married Guinevere (Guanhumara), the daughter of a noble Roman family, Arthur launched his many ships across the sea, and none could stand before his armies as he achieved the conquest of Ireland, Orkney, Gotland and Iceland. There were then twelve famous years of peace, when it seemed that all that was wise and worthy in this world might be found in Arthur's kingdom. And yet for fear of Caliburn's rusting, Arthur set out on another great campaign and soon he had subjugated the fierce kingdoms of Norway and Denmark. Still, it seemed to Arthur, these conquests were small achievements in such a large world. The great prize was before him: the wide lands of Gaul ruled by the Roman Emperor Leo. The Britons went into battle and shattered the might of the Roman Legions. Arthur laid siege to Paris and finally managed to take it.

Back at Caerleon in Britain, Arthur created an assembly of Europe, for he had now conquered the continent north of the Alps (the future empire of Charlemagne). Arthur's European vassals paid homage, as did his four vassal-kings of Albany (Scotland), Demetia (South Wales), Venedotia (North Wales) and Cornwall. But the assembly was marred by Roman demands for the surrender of Gaul and tribute payments to Emperor Leo.

Wedding of Arthur and Guinevere – the joining of two lovers was also symbolic of Arthur's conquest and unification of Britain.

War was declared and King Arthur gathered a vast army and huge fleet. He left the defence of Britain to his nephew Mordred and Queen Guinevere. As the fleet set sail, Arthur had a terrible dream about a celestial battle between a dragon and a huge bear (or, in another version, a boar). Undeterred by this disturbing dream, Arthur sailed on. His army gained victory in each battle as it drove relentlessly across Gaul. The Romans marshalled a massive army for one final conflict. Although vastly outnumbered, King Arthur's Britons crushed the imperial army, but at a cost. Thousands of Britons fell, among them many of Arthur's greatest champions, including Bedevere and Kay. However, with the Roman forces swept away, it seemed nothing could prevent Arthur's conquest of Rome itself. On reaching the Alps, however, Arthur learned that he had been deposed by Mordred, who had seized both his crown and his queen.

Arthur's forces were exhausted and diminished from their battles on the continent. But, revived by their King's wrath as well as by fresh support from the Armorica Britons, they turned toward Britain and made plans to invade their own land. On hearing of Arthur's return, Queen Guinevere fled in shame to a convent where she remained all her days. The false Mordred had gathered a great army through a godless alliance with the heathen Saxons, Germans, Scots, Picts and Irish, and all these forces awaited Arthur on the banks of the Camblam river in Cornwall. This was King Arthur's cataclysmic last battle wherein both armies were obliterated. Among those slain was Mordred and though Arthur was mortally wounded, he was carried off by the Nine Holy Women of Avalon.

The Celestial Battle – the prophetic dream of King Arthur as he left England for his continental wars, should have forewarned him of the civil war that would greet his return.

Geoffrey of Monmouth portrayed Arthur as the conqueror of the Roman Empire – long before Charlemagne established the Holy Roman Empire. Charlemagne had largely created the medieval feudal system that placed the Norman kings under the authority of both the king of France and the pope in Rome. This set-up obviously did not suit the Normans, and Geoffrey's account of Arthur's conquest of Gaul and near-conquest of Rome is essentially an attempt to establish a legal precedent for Britain's primacy over – or at least equality to – the subsequent hegemonies of the French king and the Roman papacy.

V. EXILE After Arthur's passing in 542, only ten more kings of the Britons reigned on the Island before the realm was lost. Cadwallo was the last great king to rule all Britain and, supported by the Armorica Britons, he almost restored the glory of the past. However, a plague sent from God exterminated all but a handful of the Britons. Cadwallo's son, King Cadwallader had no choice but to flee with his ships and take with him as many noble Briton survivors as he could find refuge for in Brittany. All that was noble in the British race was now in exile in Armorica and Britain lay uninhabited for eleven years. Thereafter, it was the "odious" Saxons who made an unchallenged return to Britain and found they could now take freely what they could never have won by force. The angelic voice of God, in a peal of thunder, forbade the return to Britain of the exiles until the time prophesied by Merlin: only when the mountains of Armorica erupted and Armorica itself was crowned with Brutus's diadem would the

Island of the Angles (England) again be known by Brutus's name (Britain).

Once more Geoffrey's purpose was to establish the heritage of the indomitable Britons who, after the Saxon dominion of the Island, could no longer be found in the degenerate Welsh, but only in the Armorica Britons (the Bretons of Brittany). Merlin's prophecy clearly foretold the Bretons' return to Britain. The eruption of Armorica could refer to a phenomenon such as an earth tremor or the "eruption" of Bretons and Normans marching to war. The message was obvious: God's hand took Britain from the Britons; God's hand would return it to the Breton-Normans. The "proof" of God's will was the comet that appeared in the sky during William the Conqueror's invasion.

Charlemagne – the founder of the feudal system and rival of King Arthur for the status of most famous warrior king in the literature of the Middle Ages.

Although today we see all of this as a collection of romantic fairy tales, in Geoffrey of Monmouth's time the entire feudal structure gained its legal authority through association with "fairy tale" heroes such as Charlemagne and Arthur. For five centuries after the Norman conquest, the constitutional history of Britain was basically the story of the British crown. In large part, Geoffrey of Monmouth was establishing the pedigree of the Norman kings' right to that crown – no mean feat considering the highly questionable background of William, the Norman conquerer.

Only recently descended from Viking pirates, William was not a

king, but a duke of Normandy who was a vassal of the king of France. He could not therefore claim the throne of Britain himself; as a vassal his conquest of Britain was simply an extension of his monarch's realm. Britain was technically a province of France, and the French king was the only legitimate monarch. Nor was William accepted as a true anointed king by the feudal Roman church, for besides having no claim to royal blood, he was illegitimate to boot. As a foreign French-speaking ruling class numbering only a few thousand, the Normans had a very tenuous claim to be the rightful rulers of Britain, and William's Plantagenet heirs had to struggle mightily to prove their right to the British throne. Their solution was to emphasize the Breton aspect of their Norman-Breton heritage, and then to prove a Breton link with the Celtic Britons who had inhabited England and the British Isles before the Saxon invasion. Naturally, the Plantagenets were interested in proving the historicity of King Arthur as the High King of the Britons because they based their own right to rule on proving their clear descent from this "one true king."

In the baldest propagandist terms, this was Geoffrey of Monmouth's agenda behind his compilation of *The History of the Kings of Britain*. Geoffrey's *History* established King Arthur in the popular imagination as a historical British ruler whose deeds rivalled even those of Charlemagne, the legendary but authentic historical Holy Roman Emperor. Furthermore, Geoffrey's accounts of King Arthur's mythical conquests on the European continent were

Above **Feast of the Conquerors – William and his barons ruled by force of arms.**
Right **Henry II – first of the Angevin or Plantagenet kings and a brilliant and ruthless warlord.**

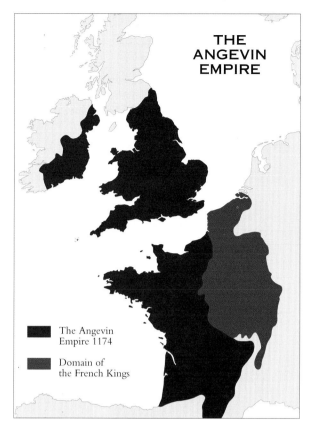

THE
ANGEVIN
EMPIRE

The Angevin
Empire 1174

Domain of
the French Kings

written for more than mere amusement. Their putative historical veracity suited the ambitions of Henry II, who eventually brought nearly all of Britain and Ireland and half the land mass of France within the boundaries of the Angevin (Plantagenet) empire.

When looking at the legend of King Arthur, we must remember the significance of this figure in the history of the British monarchy, aristocracy and clergy. As we proceed through the examination of King Arthur in his many forms, and the evolution of his legend, it becomes increasingly apparent that each of his chroniclers has interpolated elements from the politics and themes of their own time to suit their own particular purpose. As with Geoffrey of Monmouth, there was considerable manipulation (if not outright invention) of the life and history of King Arthur in order to reflect the needs of contemporary monarchs and ruling groups (such as the Cistercian monks, who saw in the legends of King Arthur an opportunity to instruct the lay public in the moral teachings of the Church). From the Norman apologists attempting to justify their right to rule Britain, to the Plantaganet Queen Eleanor of Aquitaine and her troubadours, who turned King Arthur's kingdom into a realm of courtly love, right down to the pedigree of the British Royal family of today, we shall see how the legend of King Arthur has consistently proved to be the single most important anchor for the right of monarchs to rule in Britain.

Angevin Empire – Henry II inherited from his parents vast tracts of northern France. From his uncle he inherited England and through marriage he acquired Aquitaine and most of southern France.

CHAPTER SIX

MERLIN THE MAGICIAN

I know whom thou seekest, for thou seekest Merlyn;
therefore seek no further, for I am that same Merlyn.
Le Morte d'Arthur – *Malory*

There is a peculiar "haunted" element to King Arthur's world. Even the simplest adventures have a supernatural aspect largely through the guiding spirit of Merlin the Magician, the immaculately conceived offspring of a virgin nun and a supernatural demon. His presence is felt throughout the whole body of Arthurian literature. Merlin was considered the greatest of all wizards and prophets, and was King Arthur's chief counsellor and strategist in all matters, from love to war. He was the creator of the Round Table, and the presiding intelligence behind it, and was also the architect and protector of Camelot. Half-demon, half-saint, Merlin possessed the wisdom of Solomon and the cunning of Mephistopheles. Though immortal, he had mortal feelings and failings. He was a shape-shifter and enchanter who could fly, become invisible, conjure monsters and command phantom armies. He communed with the supernatural spirits of woods, mountains and lakes, and tested his powers by duelling with other great enchanters and enchantresses. And by living both backward and forward in time, his knowledge was unsurpassed. As the poet Edmund Spenser wrote in *The Faerie Queene*:

> Merlin had in Magick more insight
> Than ever him before, or after, living wight.

As Merlin's fame spread, so did the list of his accomplishments. In time he became so intimately identified with the *spiritus mundi* of the British people that Brythonic poets often used the epithet "Clas Myrddin," or "Merlin's Enclosure," as a synonym for Britain itself. Not surprisingly, Merlin was eventually associated with that place most commonly linked to the British *spiritus mundi*: Stonehenge. The events of the legend take place just prior to Arthur's birth and in this version (which derives from Geoffrey of Monmouth), the ruling King Aurelius is a variation on the sixth-century Roman governor, Ambrosius Aurelianus.

Enchantment of Merlin – the great magician falls victim to the spells of his own apprentice, Vivien, the Lady of the Lake.

MERLIN AND THE GIANTS' RING

After King Aurelius had driven the Saxons from the land of the Britons and avenged the slaughter of his kin by the execution of both Hengist and the traitor Vortigern, his anger was quenched. He returned to his kindly nature and made generous terms of peace with his helpless foes. Also, he set about to rebuild the roads, towns and churches that the Saxons had destroyed. During these years, Aurelius came to Salisbury Plain, the site of an infamous massacre. This was the place where Hengist and the Saxons had come to make a treaty of peace with Vortigern and the Britons. But instead of peace, Hengist gave a signal and the Saxons pulled daggers from their boots and murdered no less than four hundred and sixty of the highest-ranking counts and earls of the Britons. Thinking of those martyred kinsmen, Aurelius was so moved that tears came to his eyes.

Aurelius then called forth all the people of the region and told them that some fitting memorial must be built for all these noblemen, so none might forget their sacrifice. When he had finished, one man spoke out saying, "there is no one in your kingdom who is wiser and better to seek council from than the prophet Merlin. Great are his gifts in all arts and sciences and in architecture and the use of mechanical contrivances." So the King sent his servants to find this Merlin and bring him to the court. When Merlin learned the King's wish, he spoke his mind clearly. "If you wish to bless the memory of these martyrs, you must send for the Giants' Ring which is on Mount Killaraus in Ireland. These temple stones are so large that no man of this age has the strength to move them or the wisdom to erect them. They were built by a race of giants in ancient days. But if they could be placed in position as a monument around these graves, time would have no power over them and they would

Above Stonehenge – the ancient monument and sacred site linked with the *spiritus mundi* of Britain. *Opposite* Architect of Stonehenge – Merlin's powers were said to have erected the massive structure.

stand forever." King Aurelius laughed aloud at Merlin's words. "How then can this deed be done? And why should it be done? Are we Britons so lacking in stones in our own country?" At this Merlin replied, "It can be done because I am neither of this age, nor a man. Nor are these ordinary stones, but pillars of rock locked in place by the power of ancient rites that my skill and artistry alone can release. They were brought to Ireland by a race of giants from remotest Africa. Each stone has a different medicinal property when water is poured on it; and when all the stones are gathered in one place, water from one or the other will cure every manner of illness known to man or beast." On hearing this the Britons rallied to their king, begging to be chosen for the quest. Finally the King's brother Uther Pendragon was elected to command the army that would carry out this task, but of course it was the prophet Merlin who would be the true guide.

After packing great provisions, the King's fleet put out across the sea. Receiving a fair wind they soon found themselves on the shores of Ireland and confronted by a huge army. Undaunted, Uther Pendragon attacked with such ferocity that the Irish ranks rapidly collapsed, and before the day was done, the victorious Britons marched quickly on to Mount Killaraus, where they looked in wonder at the mighty pillars of the Giants' Ring. Smiling, Merlin taunted them. "Go on, my young heroes. See if the brute strength of an army can dismantle these stones." Rising to the challenge, the troops swarmed over the stones and used every sort of device and stratagem to no avail, for they moved not one inch. Taking pity on them at last, Merlin raised his machines and ropes and levers. Then he set to work with such art and skill that he might have been shifting a pack of cards instead of dismantling a temple. Indeed, those watching him thought they must be under an enchantment, for the huge stones seemed to float across the ground and onto the ships.

When Merlin and Uther Pendragon returned to Salisbury Plain, the King greeted them warmly and all the people gathered round. The ground in which the martyrs were buried was blessed. Then Merlin raised his machines and worked his ropes and levers. Many said the giants' stones appeared — almost of their own will — to arrange themselves perfectly in a great ring around the sepulchre, just as they had been at Mount Killaraus. And the people remarked how the wizard proved that the wisdom and skill of one man was worth more than the great strength of many thousands.

This is the great Merlin the Magician who has come down to us today in countless books and tales. But has this popular image anything to do with the Dark Age warlord that we know as the historical Arthur? Indeed, was there any historical figure who could be said to be Merlin the Magician? Perversely, the answer to both questions is yes and no.

In many respects, Merlin the Magician was created by Geoffrey of Monmouth. Geoffrey's interest in Merlin spanned his writing career. His first book was the *Prophetiae Merlini*, or the *Prophecies of Merlin*, written in 1130. The *Prophecies* proved so popular that Geoffrey included them in his *History of the Kings of Britain* of 1135. The Merlin of the *History* is the fatal spirit or *deus ex machina* in the lives of Vortigern, Aurelius and Uther Pendragon. One of his greatest feats was to conduct a secret transformation of Uther at Tintagel that resulted in the conception of Arthur.

THE BIRTH OF ARTHUR

There was a war between King Uther Pendragon and his vassal the Duke of Cornwall. The cause of the war was the sea-green eyes of Igraine, the Duke's golden-haired wife. One glance into those eyes and Uther was lost, wanting nothing else but to have her near. When the Duke discovered the King's desire for his wife, he took Igraine and fled with her to Tintagel, Cornwall's strongest castle. It stood out upon a headland and could be entered only by a bridge and path so narrow that two men at arms could with ease hold its only gate against a thousand. But Uther Pendragon pursued Igraine, and as time passed he grew sick with love, and had no will to eat or fight. A kind of madness possessed him that deeply worried his men-at-arms. None had seen this iron-hard man in such a state, so one among them sent messengers to bring the great enchanter, Merlin the Wizard, for the knight believed no other might save his King. Merlin appeared suddenly, as if out of empty air, before Uther Pendragon. But when the King opened his mouth, Merlin spoke instead. "I know your heart and that it will soon burst if you do not have what you desire. And as you are the true king, I must fulfil that desire. You will lie naked this night in the pale arms of green-eyed Igraine and on this night she will conceive a child. But there is a price to be paid."

"So be it," said the King. "Tell me your price."

"The child is my price," replied Merlin. "When the child is born, he will be given to me to raise safely away from the dangers of a royal house. For I foresee a great destiny that only I may guide on its path."

Tintagel – the legendary site of the conception and birth of King Arthur, although it was built five centuries after the historical Arthur's time.

"If that is your payment," answered the Pendragon, "so shall it be. I will swear it by the life of the child."

So Merlin summoned up such powers as no other enchanter of his day possessed. There was but a wisp of mist that whirled about them, then in an instant Uther Pendragon took on the form of the noble Duke of Cornwall, and Merlin took the shape of one of the Duke's knights. Without hesitation the two, disguised, rode on to Tintagel. There the guardians at the narrow bridge opened the gate wide at the sight of their master the Duke who had come so late and unexpectedly to his Queen with but one knight-at-arms. But they did not wonder why for long, when the Duke went with so few words and so swiftly on to his wife's chamber. Strange it was that at the very moment that the Pendragon – in the Duke's form – lay transfixed by the green eyes of Igraine and within her conceived a child, the Duke of Cornwall was pierced through and slain with the lances of the King's knights. So ended the war that night. And all the Duke's lands and properties were forfeit to the crown. After a time, King Uther Pendragon returned to Tintagel and to Igraine, whom he treated with dignity and respect. He made known to her his love and in due time that love was returned, and they were wed. But thereafter, Igraine confessed to Uther that she was with child and that the father was a changeling who came to her the night of the Duke's death. Then did Uther Pendragon also make his confession, and told Igraine how Merlin had transformed him, and how he had made a bargain with the wizard. Although she was loath to give up her child, Igraine soon learned that many conspired against any Pendragon heir, so she agreed to be guided by Merlin.

Secretly in Tintagel was born a boy-child to the Queen, and as had been agreed, Merlin came in the guise of a beggar to the postern gate at night. To him was given the unchristened child, and the wizard sped away into the dark. That same night Merlin took the boy to a chapel and had him christened Arthur. Then he went to the castle of Sir Ector, who was always loyal and true to the Pendragon. It was to Sir Ector and his kind wife that Merlin brought the boy for fostering. Knowing and asking nothing of the child's paternity, Sir

Top The Wizard's Spell – by Merlin's enchantment Uther Pendragon and Igraine conceive Arthur.
Above The Price of the Spell – Uther swears to give up the child to Merlin.

Ector gladly raised Arthur well for fifteen long years. So, Arthur passed through his childhood happily, and was many times visited by the old enchanter Merlin, who became his guide and mentor. The young Arthur knew nothing of the mystery of his birth, and knew no other but Sir Ector as his father. But then after fifteen years, there came word of the death of King Uther Pendragon. Unknown even to himself, Arthur's whole life was soon destined to change far beyond the measure of his wildest dreams and strangest fantasies.

Toward the end of his life, Geoffrey returned to the subject of Merlin and composed the *Vita Merlini* or *Life of Merlin*, a Latin hexameter poem of 1528 lines about the later life and times of the magician after the events of *The History of the Kings of Britain*. Though filled with wonderful invention, the *Vita Merlini* was not conjured out of thin air. Geoffrey of Monmouth was drawing on a number of scattered sources, among them a few ancient Welsh stories. There are at least two hallowed Welsh figures on whom Geoffrey may have based his Merlin, or "Myrddin," to use its Welsh form. One is the legendary Myrddin Emrys or Merlin Ambrosius, the supernatural child-prophet summoned by Vortigern in the story of "The Red and the White Dragon." The other is the historic Myrddin ap Morfyn or Merlin Celidonius – who was also called Myrddin Wyllt or Merlin the Wild – a bard of some distinction who went mad after the Battle of Arderydd and fled to a wild forest where he lived among wild beasts. Of course, neither "Merlin" was a magician or wizard, these concepts being largely medieval. Rather, both were educated in the manner of the druids, the priestly order of the pre-Christian Celts, and were known as Vates or prophets, while the second one was also a bard, or singer-poet, of some note.

Above **The Wizard's Payment – Merlin becomes godfather and guardian of Arthur's destiny.** *Below* **The** *Life of Merlin* **reveals a complex supernatural being drawn from many sources.**

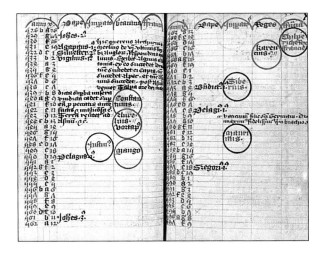

All that we know about Merlin Ambrosius is that he was the child-prophet who revealed the Red and White Dragons beneath the tower walls of doomed King Vortigern. There is some feeling that this figure is entirely legendary because in one version of the story, the demon-child is the young Dux Bellorum Ambrosius Aurelianus, and such a conflation renders the whole account rather unreliable. But of Merlin the Wild, we know substantially more. Along with Taliesin and Aneirin, he was one of the three bards of the ancient Britons. A few poems in *The Black Book of Carmarthen* are attributed to this same Merlin the Wild. Unfortunately, it is the

Merlin the Wild – the historical Merlin was Myrddin, a sixth-century Welsh bard turned mad hermit.

legendary Merlin Ambrosius (c.450–540) rather than the historical Merlin the Wild (c.540–630) whose life span might conceivably have overlapped with the historical Arthur (c.470–540). The connection between a historical Merlin and a historical Arthur appears even more tenuous when we consider that before the twelfth century neither Myrddin was connected in any way to the historical Arthur.

So, is there another source that might have suggested a relationship between Merlin and King Arthur? The answer may be found in Merlin's druid past, in the wizard archetype that he fulfils. If we look back at Teutonic mythology and the Norse *Volsunga Saga* in particular, we can clearly perceive the wizard in his primal form as the King of Gods who is also the Arch-Wizard and the One-eyed All-Father: the god Odin. Both Odin and Merlin are traditionally portrayed as long-bearded magicians. If not immortal, they are very ancient and gifted with great supernatural powers. Although they are both protectors and advisers to heroic kings, they have no interest in worldly power because they have other-worldly

concerns – Odin in Asgard, Merlin in Avalon. Merlin protects and guides Arthur and his father, Uther the Pendragon, while Odin protects and guides Sigurd and his father, Sigmund the Volsung, through many adventures and quests. Indeed, there are numerous points of congruence but the most striking relates to the claiming of a kingdom through the acquisition of an "unbreakable" hereditary sword that can cut through stone and steel. It is Merlin who sets up the contest of the Sword in the Stone that Arthur alone can claim. It is Odin who sets the contest of the Sword in the Tree that Sigmund alone can claim. Sigmund's sword breaks in battle when Odin strikes it. Arthur's breaks when he makes an unrighteous attack on a knight. Sigmund dies but when his son Sigurd is old enough, Odin asks Sigmund's

Queen to surrender the broken sword for reforging by a supernatural smith from Alfheim. Similarly, after Arthur's sword breaks, Merlin asks the Lady of the Lake to surrender another sword, forged by a supernatural smith from Avalon. The sword is named Caliburn (known in later times as Excalibur) and is claimed by Arthur.

The *Volsunga Saga* was undoubtedly a major influence on the character of our Merlin the Wizard. But there is another facet of this Merlin that is quite distinct from Odin: Merlin as magus. The messianic aspect of the magus is critical. A wizard can be destroyed; a magus in the medieval sense cannot. He can be entombed, buried or put in another dimension, but like the promise of the resurrected Christ or Arthur, the magus will return when the time is right. From the twelfth century on, Merlin became increasingly better known in the millennialist-

Opposite **Odin the All-Father – king of gods and father of the Valkyries.** *Above* **Odin the Arch-Wizard – the archetypal magician of Norse mythology and source of inspiration for the character of Merlin.**

obsessed popular mind for his prophecies than for his deeds. This Merlin the Magus became a dominant figure in popular culture that took him well beyond the realm of Arthur. Merlin was by far the most popular magus of the medieval period. As a mystical, messianic wise man, he was considered the equal of history's other great magi: Zoroaster, Moses, Solomon, Pythagoras, Jesus, Simon the Magus, Empedocles, Virgil and Faust. Until the appearance of Nostradamus in the sixteenth century, his prophecies were far more frequently consulted than any others.

By the time of Sir Thomas Malory's *Morte d'Arthur* at the end of the fifteenth century, Merlin the Magician had taken on the role of supernatur-

al wizard-mentor that has characterized him ever since. The publication of Alfred Lord Tennyson's *Idylls of the King* in the mid-nineteenth century consolidated Merlin's status as archetypal wizard, and after Tennyson, scores of Victorian artists and authors took up the image of King Arthur's mentor and forever impressed it on the public mind.

In the twentieth century, there have been thousands of variations on Merlin in books, film and television. Two of the most original are the Merlins of T.H. White's *The Once and Future King* and J.R.R. Tolkien's *The Lord of the Rings*. White's Merlin is a wonderfully eccentric absent-minded Oxford don of a wizard. He is a comic wise fool who lives backward and forward in time at once, but most of the time does not know where he is. Consequently, he is a mass of anachronisms, equally familiar with the ancient Egyptians and cricket bats. He was an ideal character to adapt to the Arthurian Disney cartoon feature, *The Sword in the Stone*. Tolkien's wizard goes by the name of Gandalf and as his Norse name suggests, he has rather more of Odin in him than does White's Merlin. He first appears as Gandalf the Grey, an amusing and wise wizard of largely human dimensions. During the course of the novel, however, he dies and is resurrected as Gandalf the White, god-like in his bearing and manner, no longer "human" but more like a supernatural force, such as destiny or fate.

In the world of film, Merlin has indeed gone backward and forward in time at once, appearing both as his ancient fifth-century druid self in John Boorman's *Excalibur* and as our era's best-known Merlin-type, the intergalactic wizard Obi-wan Konobe of George Lucas's *Star Wars*. Obi-wan Konobe acts as mentor to the young Luke Skywalker, teaching him the ways of the Force, guiding him toward his destiny as a great warrior and ultimately revealing to him the mixed blessing of his parentage. But Obi-wan cannot stay with Luke forever, and in order to

Above **Wizard of Hollywood – the magician who cast his spell in** *Excalibur* **and many other films.** *Opposite* **Merlin the Professor – T.H. White's wizard was a wise fool with an eccentric scholarly manner.**

defeat the evil Darth Vadar, the wizard must give himself up to become a part of the Force. Although he is no longer a physical presence, neither is he really gone, for he is always within Luke.

So it is with Merlin. In some versions of the story he simply vanishes. But most often he is ensnared by his own magic, frequently seduced by one of his own creatures, such as the Lady of the Lake or Morgan Le Fay. Trapped, but alive still, he exists in another dimension where he can watch or command the workings of this world, but cannot participate in them. Invisible, he can still be heard by mortals, and is available to all who desire his wise counsel.

CHAPTER SEVEN

MORGAN LE FAY

All had to marvel at the falsehoods of Morgan Le Fay;
and many knights wanted her burnt.
Le Morte d'Arthur – *Malory*

Merlin the Magician may have been the most important supernatural power behind King Arthur, but there were other significant mystical forces within the Arthurian world.

Merlin's power as an enchanter was largely rooted in the ancient tradition of male spirits, yet there was an even more ancient tradition of female spirits whose power to enchant and delude was equal to that of the master magician. In the Arthurian world, the most dangerous foes came in the least likely guises. Heroic knights who slew giants, wizards and even dragons were often entrapped by the frailest maidens. These damsels were not what they seemed, but were a knight's deadliest of foes: enchantresses and practitioners of the black arts, possessed of an unearthly beauty that was literally enthralling. They delighted in diverting chivalrous knights from their duties, tarnishing their honour and corrupting their morals. Very few knights had the strength (or even the inclination) to resist the charms of the enchantress. Unfortunately for most of them, these charms were usually short-lived, and the seduction almost always resulted in imprisonment, humiliation, torture, insanity or even death.

The greatest and most famous enchantress of all was Morgan Le Fay, the faery half-sister of King Arthur and one of the most fascinating figures in Arthurian literature. She was the beautiful and dangerous counterpart to Merlin the Magician. As Merlin was King Arthur's guardian and adviser who facilitated his rise to greatness, so Morgan was the tormentor and nemesis who engineered his downfall and the destruction of his kingdom.

Morgan had not always been the evil faery. Morgan Le Fay – or Morganna – first appeared in the twelfth century in Geoffrey of Monmouth's *Life of Merlin* as a healer without a hint of darkness about her. She was the leader of the Nine Holy Women from Avalon who came to tend Arthur's wounds after the disastrous Battle of Camlann that destroyed his kingdom. In this incarnation Morgan was not yet Arthur's

Morgan the Enchantress – Merlin's arch-rival and the architect of Camelot's destruction. She was King Arthur's faery half-sister and the greatest enchantress of her age.

sister, but she fell in love with the King and won his promise to stay with her in the realm of Avalon. Later tales reaffirmed this "original" Morgan as a mystic and a healer. However, by the end of the twelfth century, the authors of the Arthurian Romances had transformed Morgan into Arthur's

Above (top) **Morgan the Healer –**
originally a benign spirit, she came
to heal Arthur's mortal wound.
Above **Cistercian Conspiracy – the**
scribes who edited Arthurian texts
forever blackened Morgan's name.

sister, although she remained kindly and benign. But within a century or so of her conception, Morgan had turned irretrievably "bad." It was the Cistercian monks who composed the *Prose Lancelot* who forever blackened Morgan's name. Written between about 1230 and 1250, the *Prose Lancelot* (also called the *Vulgate Cycle*) was constructed around the adventures of Lancelot du Lac and the Quest for the Holy Grail.

The Cistercians were not a brotherhood to be taken lightly. Many of these zealots were not "monkish" in appearance, nor did they restrict their behaviour to prayer and study. The Templar Knights – the most feared order in the Crusades – were Cistercian warrior monks who were sworn to the holy task of exterminating infidels and heretics. Although the bookish Cistercian scribes were more subtle in their approach to semi-pagan literature than were their iron-fisted brothers in their approach to heretic cities, they were nonetheless determined to convert the Arthurian Romances into religious allegories in order to convey the superiority of the spirit over all earthly concerns. Above all, matters of the flesh were despised. Unfortunately for Morgan and her sisters, in the eyes of these churchmen "matters of the flesh" included anything female.

The Cistercians believed that it was blasphemous to attribute healing or prophetic powers to a female who was not a member of a religious order and, furthermore, that such powers under-mined the authority of the priesthood and the church. (Indeed among the Cistercians there were many monks who seriously and openly argued against the existence of the female soul.) The Cistercians set out to make Morgan as bad as they could. They twisted her ancient powers of healing and prophecy, and raised the ante by throwing demonic possession, adultery and incest into the mix. In Malory's "The Dream of the Questing Beast," Arthur, like Oedipus, has a tragic revelation of an unholy act with his sister, Morgan Le Fay.

THE DREAM OF THE QUESTING BEAST

Once went King Arthur all alone through a gentle woodland to hunt some beasts of the field. In the late afternoon, he lay down beneath a broad-leafed tree on a green knoll beside a clear deep pool. He was happy and content, but as he slept he dreamed a terrible dream of monstrous creatures like dragons and basilisks and griffons. All slithered and writhed and snapped in a great pit filled with slime. And each dragged screaming people down into that pit and slaughtered them. There were harpies and sphinxes and hydras, creatures that bore scales and fins and wings, and crawled over the earth with hooves and webs and claws. Worst of all was a monstrous serpent covered in iron scale and slime. Its nostrils flared with poisoning flame and noxious sulphur smoke. Its voice was like the baying of a pack of ravenous hounds. The creature slid out of Arthur's dream so it might come to drink at the pleasant pool. It stuck its evil fanged maw into the pool and sucked it almost dry before it slid off across the green sward into the dark wood. King Arthur shuddered with loathing. He awoke beneath his lovely tree but the limpid pool was now but a muddy hole and across the grass was a track of grease and a sulphurous stench.

The King felt as if acid had been poured on his heart, so he went to Merlin the Magician, who had greater knowledge than any man alive, and asked the meaning of his dream. Merlin told him truthfully that he had dreamed of the Questing Beast. According to Merlin, the Questing Beast was the evil spawn of a princess who wished to have an

Templar Knights – warrior monks who as crusading knights were the militant arm of the Cistercian brotherhood.

unholy union with her own brother. When the prince would not submit to her desire, the enraged princess turned her hunting hounds upon him and he was torn apart and devoured. The princess's punishment was this beast, spawned out of her sin and his blood. A monstrous and unclean creature born of monstrous vengeance and unclean desire. At this Arthur protested, for he knew of no reason for this visitation upon himself. But he soon discovered that there was in fact a stain upon his soul: when he had first met the beautiful queen of Orkney in Caerleon, they had had a great passion. And the queen had stayed with Arthur for one full month and shared his bed each night. But after that month, she suddenly told him that her passion had cooled and so she departed to her realm of Orkney.

The Questing Beast – the monstrous dream revealed the existence of the unholy, incestuously-conceived child of Arthur and Morgan Le Fay.

Only after the dream of the Questing Beast, did Arthur learn what had been conceived in that time. For now Merlin told him the truth of his own birth: that his father was King Uther Pendragon and his mother was Queen Igraine. The Queen of Orkney was in truth his half-sister Morgan Le Fay who had known all the while the story of Arthur's origin. And yet to King Arthur she had come, knowing that she was his sister, but wishing to beget an unholy child by him, for from that child she would fashion a living weapon of war and seize Arthur's kingdom. And so the child called Mordred was born, a child who was both Arthur's son and his nephew and who was destined to bring disaster to all of Britain. Such was the message of King Arthur's dream and he would keep the image of the slithering beast in his mind for all the days of his life.

In fairness, Morgan's dark side cannot be blamed entirely on the authors of the *Prose Lancelot*. For while many of her bad qualities were Cistercian inventions, still others were borrowed and adapted from earlier sources. The female figures in Camelot were almost all based on pagan queens, sibyls, priestesses and goddesses who throughout the pre-Christian world had been reputed to possess supernatural powers. But not all of these women were healers and prophets. There were priestesses among the Celts and Germans – widely known as the Angels of Death – who practiced the black arts and human sacrifice.

Aside from these mythical antecedents, there is a Dark Age contemporary of the historical Arthur who may well have served as a model for the duplicitous Morgan: the notorious poisoner, plotter and seductress Queen Brunhilda the Visigoth. It was Brunhilda who was the historical figure behind the murderous queens of the Norse *Volsunga Saga* and the German *Nibelungenlied* – epics based on the annihilation of the Rhine Burgundians in 436 by the Huns (though these epic queens also owe a debt to Hildico, the German bride of Attila the Hun who by legend murdered her husband on their wedding night). Born in AD 540, Brunhilda was married to King Sigebert of the Eastern Franks. King Sigebert's brother Chilperic was the king of the Western Franks and married Queen Brunhilda's sister. In the ensuing war between the brothers, King Sigebert was murdered through intrigue in 575, and Brunhilda was taken captive. Although her life was saved, her freedom was won by her captor's son (her nephew) who took her as his wife. She soon became a powerful force among the Franks and over the next thirty years murdered no fewer than ten kings and princes. Finally, in 613, a group of Frankish noblemen decided to put an end to her intrigues. They tortured Brunhilda for three days, had her torn apart by wild horses, and then burned her remains on a pyre.

Brunhilda's drama inspired stories in both the *Volsunga Saga* and the *Nibelungenlied*. The Volsung hero Sigmund is tricked by his sister Signi who has resolved to bear a son strong enough to murder her husband, the king of Gothland. So she secretly deceives her brother and commits incest with him. When the son grows up and – according to plan – kills the King, Signi sets a torch to the great hall. While all her in-laws burn to death, Signi confesses to Sigmund the price she has paid to exact her revenge, then she laughs and jumps into the flames herself.

In the *Nibelungenlied*, Sigfried's wife Kriemhild is furious when her brothers and cousin murder her husband. As part of her plan of vengeance, she marries mighty Attila the Hun and through seduction, sorcery,

Queen Brunhilda – the seventh-century Visigoth warrior queen, was the historical model for the murderous queens of Norse and German myth.

and bribery acquires a Hun army of her own. She invites her brothers and her cousin to a feast, but once all have gathered in the hall, the entire adult male population of her Burgundian race as well as several thousand Huns are hacked and burned to death. In exchange for having her brothers and her cousin disemboweled and decapitated, she is prepared for the price she has to pay, and willingly sacrifices her life and that of her infant son.

In these two Germanic stories, we can see the literary fruit of historical events as well as the roots of the Arthurian Morgan Le Fay. However, Celtic tradition provides another clue to Morgan's origins, linking her name with the intertwining themes of the sea, fate and the number three. In many languages Fata Morgana is a mirage that lures men to their deaths on the sea or in the desert. To the Welsh, Fata Morgana refers specifically to a mirage of a palace in the air often seen across the Straits of Messina to Anglesey. The term probably derives from the Welsh word for sea which is "mor." Similarly, sea nymphs are "mor-forwynm" and mermaids are "morgans." Was Morgan at one time a sea nymph who led sailors to their cruel fate at the bottom of the sea? Certainly there is an aspect of cruel fate to Morgan, and the name Fata Morgana strongly suggests this. In classical mythology Night and Darkness have three daughters who are known as the Fates – Birth, Life and Death. In Greek the Fates were called the Moerae and the leader of the Fates was known as the Moeragetes, or the Fata Moeragetes. In the traditional folklore of European cultures, the Three Fates appear on the last day of a person's life and escort him from this world to the next, just as Morgan was one of the three queens who appeared to the dying Arthur on the battlefield at Camlann. The figure of Morgan is also seen in the Celtic Triple goddess whose three faces – Morrigan, Macha and Bodbh – signify birth, life and death.

Goddess, healer, sister, lover, plotter, avenger, seductress – the character of Morgan Le Fay has travelled great distances. There is no doubt that her good name was cruelly (and irreparably) slandered by the Cistercians. But then again, perhaps it's just as well. Beyond being an interesting comment on male paranoia in the Middle Ages, the resulting portrait has endured as one of literature's most complex and fascinating women. Morgan is the enchantress whose outlines are still reflected in the images of Lucrezia Borgia, Mata Hari and Eva Peron.

Three Sisters: the Moerae or Fates – the three faces of Fata Morgana, a manifestation of the triple goddess linked to birth, life and death.

CHAPTER EIGHT

THE LADY OF THE LAKE

"That is the Lady of the Lake," Merlin said to Arthur.
"Within the lake is a rock and therein is hidden a land both rich and fair."
Le Morte d'Arthur – *Malory*

 Among the many enchantresses of Camelot, only one dared challenge the infamous Morgan Le Fay. That honour belonged to the Lady of the Lake. Variously named Vivien, Vivienne, Niniane or Nimue, this elusive enchantress gave King Arthur his magic sword Excalibur. She also fostered Lancelot du Lac, training him to be the greatest knight of the age, then sending him to defend Camelot.

Born to a magical kingdom beneath her enchanted lake, this wild and beautiful spirit was the most beloved disciple of Merlin the Magician – although she later cast a spell on her former master thereby depriving Camelot of its greatest protector. Even so, perhaps through Merlin's influence, Vivien became concerned with the fate of King Arthur and committed to the well-being of Camelot and its mortal inhabitants. Indeed, after Merlin's departure, the Lady of the Lake became King Arthur's chief adviser and Camelot's guardian spirit.

The portrayal of Vivien as Arthur's protector varied from story to story. In some accounts, the king is so disaster-prone that the Lady of the Lake appears to be more of a full-time bodyguard than a guiding spirit. At other times she spends most of her days simply neutralizing Morgan Le Fay's evil magic and vengeful deeds, including several outright assassination attempts. One of the more spectacular and creative attempts on Arthur's life involved a magnificent jewelled cape that according to Malory's *Morte d'Arthur* Morgan gave Arthur. Indeed, had it not been for the timely intervention of the Lady of the Lake, the *Morte d'Arthur* would have been a very short book indeed.

Above **Wise Counsel – the Lady of the Lake and Merlin advise King Arthur.** *Opposite* **Spell of the Enchantress – the temptations of nymphs could be a blessing or a curse.**

THE JEWELLED CAPE

To the court of Camelot one bright winter morning, came a fair young damsel dressed in virgin white. This lady-in-waiting to Morgan Le Fay had come at the bidding of her mistress to wish King Arthur good health and to bring him a fair gift as a token of Morgan's love. The lady said that her mistress had heard that many within Camelot spoke evil of her and had tried to prove that she conspired against the King. She told Arthur and his court, "My mistress, Queen Morgan, wants you to know that all the evils you may have heard about her are jealous lies. My mistress holds nothing but love and loyalty for Arthur who is to her both brother and king." There was murmuring about the hall, with many whispers of disbelief and concern among those who knew of Morgan's stratagems. But none spoke up against the lady, for it was known that King Arthur would hear nothing against his sister. The King accepted the greeting with kindness and good grace and Morgan's lady proceeded to have a servant bring to her a trunk out of which she took a great cape fit for an emperor or a god. It was made of silk and velvet, all embroidered with golden threads, lined with ermine fur and set all over with the richest gems that had ever been seen in Camelot.

"Your sister Morgan Le Fay sends this mantle to the King, so whatever offence she may have caused will in some part be forgiven," said Morgan's lady holding the glimmering cape over her outstretched arms.

"Tell my kind sister," responded Arthur warmly, "that though there is no need for so great a gift, I will receive it with delight in the love it conveys."

"Thank you my lord, but my mistress made me promise that I would place this mantle with my own hands upon your shoulders," said the lady in white, smiling and speaking with so gentle a voice, "and that after so doing, would speak this blessing to you: my lord, when you feel this rich mantle's warmth, think only how true your sister's love for her King."

King Arthur was about to get up from his throne and receive his sister's blessing. But in that moment, a pale hand was placed lightly upon his sleeve and he found that he could not rise. The hand was that of the Lady of the Lake who was sitting with a few other ladies and servants upon the steps of the dais around the throne. Looking down into Vivien's face, he smiled a kindly smile and, showing no concern that others might perceive, he leaned over to her. And as Vivien whispered in his ear, the smile faded from the King's face. Without expression, the king looked on the gentle smile and pretty face of the maid in white who now held out to him his sister's gift of the jewelled cape. But then, slowly, he smiled again and spoke.

"I am truly overwhelmed by this magnificent gift," said Arthur. "But do me one kind favour and place it first on your own shoulders. Then whirl once or twice about, so I might see all the mantle's jewels in full display."

"But my lord, I dare not," the lady protested mildly and yet she still kept that child's innocent smile upon her lips. "It would not be seemly for me to wear a king's garment."

"It would if the king so wished it," said Arthur.

"My King, I cannot. I will not!" cried the lady. Her smile was gone, as was her look of innocence. Her face showed now that she knew well what in Morgan's name she had delivered to the King. Arthur's face was grim. But now, the Lady of the Lake stood tall by his throne. She was silent for a moment as she looked straight into the eyes of Morgan's maid. Then she spoke. "You will grant the King his wish," was all Vivien said.

The maid in white spoke not a word. She put the mantle upon her own shoulders and at once dropped down dead. The jewelled cape's poison seared her bones and the gemstones became hot coals that burned her flesh. The mantle became a robe of flame that consumed everything within. All that remained was cinder. Then there was heard a scream so hideous that all understood this could only be the spirit of a demon being dropped into the pit of hell. All in the court of Camelot stood in silence and horror. Some shuddered at the thought of what might have been, but for the Lady of the Lake.

The first to speak was the King himself, but his words were those of Morgan, now filled with sad irony: "When you feel this rich mantle's warmth, think only how true your sister's love for her King."

Guide and Protectress – the Lady of the Lake warns her King, not for the first or the last time, of an attempt upon his life.

"Alas, my lord," said Vivien with pain in her voice. "Sadly, you have learned at last the true nature of your sister's love for her King."

Like Morgan Le Fay, the Lady of the Lake is a complex character drawn from many traditions, and in both her and Morgan we find something of the old Celtic water deities – ghostly spirits known as the "White Ladies" –

Top **Enthralment – the fragile beauty of cruel nymphs destroyed the spirit of many a brave knight.**
Above **Gift of the Sword – the Lady of the Lake conjures up the weapon that will grant Arthur victory.**

who were found in sacred fountains, lakes, rivers and grottoes. To reach the kingdoms of these beings it was necessary to pass through or across water. Their palaces, spectacular magical structures of ivory and gold that glowed with light, could be found in caves far beneath a lake or a river, or in the waves of the sea.

In Welsh folklore, there are several kinds of related water spirits. One is called the Tylwyth Teg (literally "beautiful ancestry") and another is called the Gwagged Annwn ("other-world glamour"). Both Tylwyth Teg and Gwagged Annwn were pale-skinned and possessed an otherworldly beauty. The Tylwyth Teg were more often dark-haired, while the Gwagged were nearly always blonde. Charming as they were, it was advisable to avoid the Tylwyth Teg, who were inclined to steal unattended babies, or kidnap mortal adults for terms lasting anywhere between seven years and a hundred. It was far safer to stick with the

fair-haired Gwagged Annwn, who were generous and frequently married mortal men, the union often resulting in gifted beings with magical powers. Morgan seems to fit best into the Tylwyth category, while Vivien better suits the Gwagged Annwn, particularly as tradition has it that there were male Gwagged Annwn as well. Not so numerous as their female counterparts, these male spirits were always old with long beards, while their consorts remained ever-young. In this classic May-December coupling there is an echo of the relationship between Vivien and Merlin.

Although the Gwagged Annwn were preferable to the Tylwyth Teg, even "good" water nymphs could behave in ways confounding to mortals: the Lady of the Lake gave Arthur Excalibur, protected Camelot and the king with her enchantments and reared Lancelot, but she also had a part in Arthur's downfall by removing Merlin from his realm (and from our own). What crime did Merlin commit to deserve such a fate? Was it the price he had to pay for Arthur's sword? Or had he broken some ancient taboo? In most versions of the story – including this one from the *Prose Lancelot* – no answer is given.

Enchanted Forest – over the ages, the Arthurian landscape became increasingly over-populated by nymphs, fairies, elves and imps.

Above and opposite The Enchanter
Enchanted – subtle as the play of light on water,
the Lady enthralls the master magician.

THE ENCHANTMENT OF MERLIN
THE MAGICIAN

In his early years, Merlin's powers were great enough to command all the ladies of the lake and bend them to his will. But as he grew older, he taught his pupil Vivien more and more of his spells. So, it was she who grew stronger with time. And eventually so adept was she, that even the great Merlin became bewitched by her wit and artful beauty. True to the way of enchantresses, Vivien wheedled out of him all the wizard might teach her of magic. As she grew more powerful, Merlin became more obsessed. When at last she believed she could learn no more from her master, she lured Merlin into the enchanted forest of Brocielande in Brittany and had him rest beneath a thorn tree.

There she sang a song that was a sleeping spell and Merlin fell into a trance. Then she trailed her wimple nine times around the thorn tree under which the magician lay. And so the enchantress Vivien built a tower of air from which Merlin could never emerge. From this place and its enchanted tower, Vivien could come and go as she pleased, but to all others it was invisible. However, it is said to this day that a voice may be heard by those who wander in the ancient wood of Brocielande - the faint and distant voice of Merlin among the branches of the trees calling out and bewailing his fate.

The character of the capricious water spirit can also be traced to Greek mythology, which had a profound influence on Arthurian literature. The Greeks had hundreds of demi-sea gods and water nymphs. The nymphs, known as Naiads, were for the most part healers and nurturers who inspired, helped and protected mortals (although some, like the Limnads of lakes, marshes and swamps were neither trustworthy nor wholesome). There are so many similarities between the Greek Naiads and the Arthurian Ladies of the Lake that it is inconceivable that the former did not in some part inspire the latter.

The most important Naiads were the nine water nymphs called the Muses. In Arthurian mythology, the most important water spirits were the nine water nymphs who were called the Ladies of the Lake. And just as it was one of the Nine Muses who presented the hero Perseus with his super-natural sword, so it was one of the Ladies of the Lake who presented Arthur with his sword Excalibur. In Greek legends, the Muses are interchangeable with the Nine Daughters of the Hesperides, an earthly paradise in the western sea where the Apples of Immortality grow. In Arthurian legends, the Nine Lake Ladies appear to be identical with the Nine Ladies of Avalon (which means "Isle of Apples"), also an earthly paradise in the western sea. The first of the nine Greek Muses (and in some accounts, their mother) was Mnemosyne ("memory"), which is usually short-ened to Mneme. In Arthurian literature, the first of the Ladies of the Lake was frequently called

Venus and the Muses – the Ladies of the Lake of ancient times: the Nine Daughters of the Hesperides and guardians of the sacred fountains of inspiration and immortality.

Nimue. As phonetic transliterations, the Greek "Mneme" and Celtic "Nimue" are one and the same name.

And of the Lady of the Lake's other name, Vivien, is there a classical connection there too? Perhaps, for Vivien is thought to be a northern Celtic name that was adapted by writers of the Arthurian Romances from the Roman-Celtic water goddess known to Roman writers as Covianna. (The Latin "Co-Vianna" transforms into the Celtic "Vi-Vianna" or Vivien.) Not so grand a goddess as the Olympian Muses, Covianna was known well enough in her time. In Roman-Celtic Britain, Covianna shrines were small wells where offerings were commonly made. Celts made votive offerings while the Roman soldiers threw coins. In fact, this ancient practice is the basis for our own tradition of the wishing well and it seems that Covianna, the spirit of the wishing well, is that entity called "Lady Luck." A shrine to Covianna may still be seen on Hadrian's wall, where she was worshipped by the Roman Legionnaires and perhaps even by the historical Arthur's Sarmatian cavalrymen.

Still, however illustrious her pedigree, the Lady of the Lake and her sister nymphs remain strangely ambivalent creatures. They had their own sense of book-keeping, and what they gave, they might well take away; their gifts and blessings were always something of an illusion. A knight encountering such a being, would do well to tread carefully, because no matter how alluring the lady might seem, one could never be sure what kind of spirit she was, nor where such an encounter would lead. In his haunting "La Belle Dame Sans Merci," the nineteenth-century English poet John Keats wrote of a knight who failed to take the proper precautions when dealing with a lady of the lake.

STONE STELE DEDICATED TO THE WATER-GODDESS

Left Lady Luck – an ancient Roman relief of the goddess Covianna.
Above **Rhine Maidens – river nymphs who entice their victims with languid song, before dragging them down to a watery grave.**

LA BELLE DAME SANS MERCI

O, what can ail thee, knight-at-arms,
Alone and palely loitering?
The sedge has withered from the lake,
And no birds sing.

O, what can ail thee, knight-at-arms,
So haggard and so woe-begone?
The squirrel's granary is full,
And the harvest's done.

I see a lily on thy brow,
With anguish moist and fever dew;
And on thy cheeks a fading rose
Fast withereth too.

I met a lady in the meads,
Full beautiful - a faery's child,
Her hair was long, her foot was light,
And her eyes were wild.

I made a garland for her head,
And bracelets too and fragrant zone;
She looked at me as she did love,
And made sweet moan.

I set her on my pacing steed
And nothing else saw all day long;
For sidelong would she bend and sing
A faery's song.

She found me roots of relish sweet,
And honey wild and manna dew;
And sure in language strange she said –
"I love thee true".

She took me to her elfin grot,
And there she wept and sighed full sore,
And there I shut her wild wild eyes
With kisses four.

And there she lulled me asleep,
And there I dreamed – Ah! woe betide
The latest dream I ever dreamed
On the cold hill side.

I saw pale kings and princes too,
Pale warriors, death-pale were they all:
They cried – "La belle Dame sans Merci
Hath thee in thrall!"

I saw their starved lips in the gloam,
With horrid warning gaped wide,
And I awoke and found me here
On the cold hill's side.

And this is why I sojourn here
Alone and palely loitering,
Though the sedge is withered from the lake,
And no birds sing.

So for one and all, the gifts and blessings of water spirits were always something of an illusion. These spirits of lakes and fountains are the symbolic
source of life, health, wealth and inspiration. However, there is always an
element of danger. We will never control them. At least we know a few of
their names, and that brings a little understanding. It explains why the
Enchantress Nimue-Vivienne (Luck and Inspiration) would struggle against
the Enchantress Morgan Le Fay (Fate and Delusion). But by whatever
name, they will always remain as elusive as their
watery spirits.

**La Belle Dame Sans Merci – a
knight held in thrall by the beautiful
child of a faery.**

CHAPTER NINE

EXCALIBUR

In the midst of the lake Arthur saw an arm clothed in
white samite, that held a fair sword in its hand.
Le Morte d'Arthur – *Malory*

 The sword Excalibur was the gift of the Lady of the Lake to King Arthur. Its blade was unbreakable and could easily cleave steel and stone without being blunted. It shone like a torch in battle and when Arthur carried it, he could not be defeated. Its jewelled scabbard had a magical property that prevented the warrior who wore it from being wounded. This was not the sword that Arthur drew from the stone to prove he was the true king. That sword, one legend tells us, was broken during an unrighteous duel with King Pellinore in which Arthur violated his lawful authority as king. Only Merlin's intervention – he cast a spell on Pellinore – saved the King's life. After this episode, Merlin took Arthur in search of another sword, one with which he might regain his authority and fulfil his destiny. In this story from Malory, the two travel to the realm of the Lady of the Lake where Arthur is given Excalibur and its scabbard, making him both ever-victorious and invulnerable.

EXCALIBUR AND THE LADY OF THE LAKE

One day Merlin took King Arthur into the wilderness, to a lake both broad and fair, and the magician told the King to go and stand by the lake and look out upon it. As Arthur looked, he saw a miraculous sight: a maid's pale arm clothed in white samite holding aloft in her hand a gleaming sword. Then, too, Arthur was amazed to see a damsel as beautiful as a pagan goddess who walked toward him over the rippling lake, as if it were a paved road.

"What damsel is this?" asked Arthur.

"This is the Lady of the Lake," said Merlin. "This lake is her domain, for beneath the lake is a great rock and within that rock is a realm as rich and fair as any on earth. In that realm within the rock is to be found her palace all filled with wondrous gifts."

"And what of this sword?" asked Arthur.

"This is the Lady's sword of destiny that awaits its true master. It

is the best sword in the world. So you must speak to the Lady of the Lake and make whatever pledge she may ask, if she will offer it to you. For she alone will judge whether you are worthy enough to carry it like a torch into the world." Arthur turned to speak to the Lady who stood before him on the lake like a shimmering vision.

"My Lady of the Lake," said Arthur, "tell me what sword this is that is held aloft in the midst of your lake. For I am told there is no other like it in this world and I would have it for my own."

"This is the sword Excalibur that was made for one hand alone to take into the world," said the Lady of the Lake. "Are you the one true king who has come? Are you the one named Arthur?"

"I am Arthur the King," he replied.

"Then I will make you a gift of this sword for your destiny is forged within its blade," said the Lady. "But for this you must swear to grant me whatever gift I may wish from you in time to come."

"I so swear," said King Arthur.

"Then take yourself to that barge on the lake edge," said the Lady, "and cross over to where the hand holds the sword aloft. There take Excalibur and the jewelled scabbard also. But guard it well, for your life and it are bound as one for all the days of your life."

Excalibur – the gift of the Lady of the Lake to Arthur. It was the finest sword in the world, for any who held it was victorious.

So Arthur and Merlin went to the barge and crossed over the lake to the hand that held the shining sword aloft. Then Arthur grasped the sword and the scabbard as well. The miraculous hand released its grip and vanished into the depths of the lake. Arthur

looked upon the blade of Excalibur that was so wonderfully fashioned and saw that its grip was made to fit his hand perfectly. He saw too the beautifully wrought scabbard, which was set with many precious gemstones.

"Which do you like best," asked the wise Merlin, "the sword or the scabbard?"

"I like the sword best," replied Arthur without hesitation.

"I don't doubt it, but the scabbard is the greater gift and is worth ten of those swords," said Merlin. "So long as you have the scabbard on you, you shall lose no blood and never be wounded. Therefore keep it with you always."

Arthur placed the sword Excalibur within its scabbard and bound it to his side. Looking across the lake he saw no sign of the Lady or the hand that had held the sword. So with Merlin, Arthur brought the barge ashore, then they mounted their horses and rode away toward the kingdoms of mortal men.

Curiously, in the earliest histories and legends of Camelot and King Arthur, there is no record of the king being given a sword by the Lady of the Lake. In these early accounts, Arthur's sword is called Caliburn (or, in Welsh, Caledfwich). Both names are derived from the old Irish Caladbolg, which means "flashing sword." The name Excalibur resulted from the first French versions of Arthurian stories in which the authors transformed the Celtic name Caliburn to one more suited to Norman French: Excalibur. It was not until the French Arthurian Romances of the late twelfth century that Excalibur came to be the gift of the Lady of the Lake to Arthur. It is very likely, however, that the source of this legend comes from myths and traditions that are much older than even the earliest Arthurian tales.

Left **Hidden Properties – Arthur was told that the secret of his destiny was forged in Excalibur's blade.**
Above **Testing the Sword – Sigurd the Volsung's magic sword was forged by the master smith of Alfheim.**

We have already explored some of the links between King Arthur and the Norse *Volsunga* heroes. In both traditions, it was the young hero's acquisition of a sword that signified his right to rule. Furthermore, both swords – the one that Arthur pulled from the stone as well as the one Sigmund pulled from the tree – were broken in battle and needed to be replaced. These "second swords" (Arthur's Excalibur and Sigurd's Gram) also had much in common. To claim Excalibur, Merlin instructed Arthur to go to the Lady of the Lake, the keeper of a sword that was forged by an elf smith of Avalon. Similarly, Odin instructed Sigurd (Sigmund's son) to go to his mother, the keeper of the fragments of his father's sword that had been reforged by an elf smith of Alfheim. Both their swords were

King Arthur in Battle – with Excalibur, the king was able to strike down and defeat any foe who challenged him.

unbreakable, unbluntable and unbeatable. Arthur's sword had a scabbard which would not permit any weapon to draw his blood. Sigurd gained similar invulnerability when he bathed in the blood of a dragon he had slain with his sword, Gram. The immunity granted both heroes was lost through the betrayal of women. Sigurd was betrayed by a lover who revealed to his

assassin the vulnerable spot where the dragon blood had not touched him. Arthur was betrayed by Morgan who stole both sword and scabbard, replacing them with counterfeit versions. Eventually, Excalibur was retrieved, but tragically the scabbard was lost forever.

Of course, King Arthur and Sigurd were not the only heroes with supernatural swords. By the time of the French Romances, most kings and heroes around whom legends grew possessed swords with magical properties: the great emperor Charlemagne's sword was Joyeuse; the Spanish epic hero El Cid had a sword that bore the name Tizona; the national hero of Denmark, Holger Dansk – also known as Ogier the Dane – carried the sword Courtain; the Rhineland hero Siegfried brandished Balmung and the Ostrogoth champion Dietrich von Berne wielded Mimung. All these swords have the same source as Excalibur: an elf smith known by as many names as there are tales. Among the Saxons and early English he was called Wayland the Smith. The Germans called him Wieland and the Norse, Volund. Whatever the name, his origin was the

Above **Thetis the Water Nymph – she presented her son Achilles with the god-forged sword and armour.** *Below* **Vulcan – the crippled and stunted smith at his forge.**

Roman god Vulcan, who was modelled on the Greek god Hephaestus, the master smith whose forge was beneath the volcano of Aetna.

Hephaestus forged the armour and weapons of the two classical heroes, Perseus and Achilles. However, neither of them acquired their weapons and armour directly from the smith-god. Perseus received his through the offices of the water nymphs known as the Nine Muses. Achilles was armed by his mother, the sea nymph Thetis. And just as Arthur received Excalibur from the Lady of the Lake, many of the Germanic heroes were given their weapons by the Rhine maidens, river nymphs known as the Nixies. The Norse heroes were armed by Swan maidens, water nymphs who transformed themselves into the Valkyries, Odin's battle maidens.

By the early thirteenth century, the story of Excalibur as the gift of the Lady of the Lake was well-established. The tale of Excalibur's return after the Last Battle appeared at this time as well. In the first written versions, Arthur ordered a knight called Girflet to cast Excalibur into an enchanted pool. The knight came to be variously identified as Galahad, Perceval or even Lancelot, but most commonly – as in this tale from Malory – the chosen knight was Sir Bedevere.

Ride of the Valkyries – the Norse battle maidens who carry slain heroes to Odin's hall of Valhalla.

EXCALIBUR'S RETURN

Upon the dread carnage of that last battle of Camlann where all the flower of Britain's knighthood perished, there remained alive just two knights, Sir Bedevere and his lord and master, King Arthur. But Arthur had received a terrible mortal wound and he could not raise himself. So, as the light was fading upon the battleground, he commanded Bedevere to do what must be done, but what he could not himself achieve.

"Take my great sword Excalibur," said the King with rasping breath, "and carry it beyond this bloodstained ground to beyond that hill where you will find a deep lake. There I command you to throw Excalibur into its midst. When this is done, come and tell me what you have seen."

"I will do as you command, my lord," said Bedevere to his King. With good intent he went away with the sword Excalibur, but on his way he saw the glint of its jewelled pommel that was like the red eye of a dragon, and the sheen of its blade that was like a blue flame. As he approached the lake he thought how great the loss of this sword would be and how in the hand of a true knight many evils might yet be overcome. What good, he thought to himself, would come from its loss? None he could image. So he hid Excalibur beneath a tree by the water's edge.

"What saw you upon the lake?" asked the wounded King when Bedevere returned to the dread battleground.

"My lord," said Bedevere, "I saw nothing but the waves and heard nothing but the wind."

"Then you have been untrue and have

Sir Bedevere – as he hurled Excalibur into the water, he was amazed to see a hand rise up and grasp the sword.

not achieved the deed," said Arthur. "Go again and do as your King has commanded you to do."

Sir Bedevere turned again from the battleground and went to the lake beyond and in shame took up the sword, but again the red jewel glinted in the pommel and the light shone upon the long blade. Again he was tempted to save the sword, so he hid it beneath the tree.

"What saw you upon the lake?" asked the King when Bedevere returned for the second time.

"My lord," said Bedevere, "I saw nothing but the waves and heard nothing but the wind."

"Then you have been untrue and have not achieved the deed," said Arthur. "Go again and do as your King commands."

Sir Bedevere turned yet again from the battleground and went to the lake beyond and in shame took up the sword, but this time he closed his eyes so that they could not look upon the red jewel or the silver blade. Thus, Sir Bedevere kept his resolve to serve his lord and he wrapped the blade around with its belt and hurled it with all his strength out to the midst of that lake.

All astonished was Bedevere when he saw that out of the lake came an arm in white samite whose hand caught the sword from the air and held it aloft and still. The hand brandished the sword three times, then both hand and sword disappeared into the water.

"What saw you upon the lake?" asked the wounded King, when Bedevere returned once more to the dread battleground.

"My lord," said Bedevere, "I saw a hand and arm in white samite rise out of the lake and catch the sword. Then the hand thrice brandished Excalibur. Three times it encircled the air and in that moment vanished away both hand and sword beneath the water."

"Then you have been true and achieved the deed," said Arthur, "as your King commanded."

And all about the battlefield was deadly still, as the light faded from the sky and the dark of night came on.

The symbolism of the sword surrendered is universally understood as an acknowledgment of defeat and is often emblematic of death. However, King Arthur's careful return of Excalibur to the lake suggests something quite specific: a sacrifice or a votive offering made to fit a cult ritual. For in the story of Excalibur we find the relic of an ancient "ritual sacrifice of the sword" to a deity of a sacred lake or spring. Nor are the three requests, three returns and three flourishes arbitrary details; rather they are elements of a sacred formula, the ritual of the thrice-asked question and third-time-lucky answer beloved of myths and fairy tales, from Oedipus to

Rumpelstiltskin. In the return of Excalibur to the sacred lake we are seeing devotees on a mission of sacrifice. It is repeated until the task is done and the ancient ritual completed.

Such offerings at sacred lakes and grottoes were common among the Celts and Germans; hundreds of votive swords have been found in pools and lakes throughout Europe. Some sword rituals also involved blood sacrifices – both animal and human – which were followed by the symbolic washing away of the blood of guilt. In the hands of the priestess, a bloodied sword would be retrieved and cleansed, then given life again through a formal presentation. This was the symbolic importance of Excalibur: the ceremonial presentation and the ritual sacrifice of the sword, its birth, its drowning and its eventual rebirth...which we await still.

Excalibur's Blade – the sword still shimmers in the imagination. To this day there are those who swear they have seen an arm in white samite holding the blade aloft in the gentle mist of dawn or the silver haze of moonlight.

CHAPTER TEN

CAMELOT AND THE ROUND TABLE

In Camelot no man shall take to battle in a wrongful quarrel for no law, nor for world's goods. Unto this were all the knights sworn of the Table Round.
Le Morte d'Arthur – *Malory*

Just as the sword Excalibur was the ideal weapon of the age, so King Arthur's realm of Camelot was the ideal kingdom, a medieval Utopia governed by King Arthur and the Knights of the Round Table. The great castle walls and white beacon towers of Camelot shone out over the barbaric war-torn lands of a tumultuous world. Camelot was an idyllic realm where just laws were enforced by powerful and devout knights motivated by the highest ideals.

King Arthur's Camelot was shaped largely by the dual conventions of the chivalric code and courtly love. In Camelot, these conventions were indelibly dramatized by stories of knights who ventured forth from Camelot to impose Christian virtue on a hostile world – or, on other occasions, to rescue a beautiful maiden who had fallen into the wrong hands. Taken from the *Prose Lancelot*, the adventure of Sir Gareth at Castle Perilous is a playful romance for the court's entertainment, but at the same time, it functions as a primer for young men learning the chivalric code.

CASTLE PERILOUS

A damsel called Linet once came to Camelot seeking a champion who might rescue her sister, the lovely Lady Lyonesse, who had for two years been besieged in her Castle Perilous by the Knight of the Red Lands. King Arthur immediately granted Linet's petition, but she was outraged when, instead of a famous knight, Arthur chose an eager kitchen knave. Unknown to any in Camelot, the young man was in fact Gareth of Orkney, the brother of Sir Gawain and youngest nephew of Arthur. Throughout their journey Linet reviled Gareth at every opportunity; she even mocked the worthy foes he defeated along the way! When at last they arrived at Castle Perilous, they found hanging from the trees forty unfortunate knights who had previously undertaken this quest. Undeterred by their cruel death,

Camelot – knights from all over Christendom came to King Arthur's court hoping to become one of the Knights of the Round Table.

Gareth sounded a great ivory horn which hung from a sycamore tree. Straight-away the huge Red Knight charged out to answer the challenge, his helmet, armour, shield, lance and even his steed all of the bloodiest red. For the better part of a day Gareth and the Red Knight fought in the little vale under the castle wall, where all within might see the battle. The lovely Lady of Lyonesse was one of the most breathless spectators. Eventually Gareth overpowered his opponent, splitting his helmet and knocking him to the earth. Only his merciful nature stopped him from taking the Red Knight's life. The Knight,

acknowledging defeat, promised to withdraw his forces and go to Arthur's court so that he might swear his allegiance to the King. Thus the siege of Castle Perilous was raised by the honourable kitchen knave. Gareth's true identity was revealed and he and Lady Lyonesse, having fallen deeply in love, plighted their troth together.

Once the lovers had sworn to marry, their passion for each other was so strong that that very night the Lady Lyonesse came to Gareth in his bed chamber. But their dalliance was soon interrupted by the entrance of an armed knight accompanied by a great clamour and many strange glittering lights. The intruder attacked Gareth and wounded him in the thigh, but Gareth swiftly grabbed his sword

Above Slain Knights – the victims of the Knight of the Red Lands.
Opposite Sir Gareth – by his victory over the Red Knight, Gareth won the heart of the Lady Lyonesse.

and struck the knight's head off. While Gareth's wound was being staunched, there appeared in his chamber the damsel Linet, ever-vigilant of her sister's virtue. She swiftly picked up the unknown knight's head, applied an ointment, then replaced the head on the fallen body. Immediately the knight returned to life, albeit somewhat shaken, and she led him away.

The next night, the same thing happened. Once more the lovers were prevented from dishonouring themselves by the ferocious knight. This time, however, Gareth cut the head of his assailant into a hundred pieces and threw them from the window. Linet patiently collected the pieces and, applying the ointment as before, reassembled the head and restored the knight to life. The wounds suffered by Gareth in these encounters not only further delayed the lovers, but could only be healed by the lady whose enchantments had caused them. However, Linet saw to it that he was in full health again in time for his wedding, after which the phantom chaperone left the lovers in peace, his restless moral spirit soothed by the lawful union.

Although "Castle Perilous" is set in a distant realm, the story demonstrates that in Arthur's time, it was the kingdom of Camelot that stood for justice and order. It was to the Round Table that a young woman went if she was in need of a brave champion to rescue her sister. In fact, most of the Arthurian tales take place away from Camelot; the realm itself is rarely described in the literature. If Camelot was a medieval Utopia, then we must remember that Utopia is a Greek word meaning "no place." The location and nature of Camelot shift according to the time in which it is being chronicled, just as the attributes of King Arthur are adapted to suit the aspirations of each age.

The Camelot we have come to know seems to be the invention of the late twelfth-century French Romances, although nearly every region of Britain claims to be the home of this fabled realm – Carlisle in Cumbria, Camelon in Scotland, Chester in the Midlands, Caerleon in Wales, Camelford in Cornwall and Cadbury Castle in Somerset, to name but a few. At the end of the thirteenth century, however, Winchester Castle in Wessex was widely accepted as the site of the real Camelot. Certainly the castle had the most remarkable relic to reinforce its claim – the Round Table itself, which still hangs in Winchester's Great Hall. The most famous of all Arthurian relics, the solid oak table is eighteen feet in diameter and weighs one and a quarter tons. The table top is painted with alternating green and white spokes to mark a place for each of Arthur's knights. But however magnificent, the Winchester Round Table is a medieval forgery. Forensic examination indicates that the wood was cut for this table just before 1250 – or seven centuries after the historical Arthur's time. Even so, the table does tell the story of King Arthur, for in its history we can see the fluctuating fortunes of the Arthurian myth and its relationship to the British crown.

The Winchester Round Table was probably made during the reign of Edward I (1239-1307), one of the most accomplished of the royal Arthurian enthusiasts. He not only "reclaimed" the Round Table but, in 1282 he acquired an ancient "Crown of King Arthur" surrendered by the Welsh after the death of the last native Welsh prince. Understanding the symbolic force of such relics, Edward arranged for his son to wear this crown, and in so doing the future Edward II became the first Prince of Wales. This established a royal sequence of titles

Above **Winchester Round Table – the massive medieval oak table that still hangs in the castle's Great Hall. *Opposite* Camelot – a vision of the white towers of the medieval Utopia.**

for the heir to the British throne that was meant to emulate the various stages in the life of Arthur and is still in use today: at birth the prince is baptized the Duke of Cornwall (Arthur was born in Cornwall); in adolescence he is crowned the Prince of Wales (at fifteen Arthur was chosen to be the ruler of the Welsh-Britons); when the reigning monarch dies, the Prince of Wales becomes king of England (as Arthur presided over all the people of Britain during his reign).

After Edward I, the connection between the royal family and King Arthur via the Round Table was continually reinforced. In 1344, Edward III vowed to establish a new Order of the Round Table. He commissioned a huge stone Round Table Hall, but unfortunately, both the hall and the order were cancelled when Edward III heard the French king had already embarked on a similar project. (In its place, Edward established the Order of the Garter and this exclusive knighthood – its membership is set at twenty-six – continues to this day.) Following the War of the Roses (1450-85), the Tudor royal family seized on the Round Table tradition as a means of drawing together the many political factions of the country under one ruler. In 1516 the Round Table at Winchester was painted and indeed we can see the downfall of the Stuart kings, the rise of Cromwell and the return of the monarchy directly reflected in its physical condition. Close examination reveals that major restoration work was needed because the table was full of holes, most of which were densely clustered around the image of Arthur's head and the centre of the Tudor Rose. These were bullet holes acquired in 1645 when Cromwell's troops used the Round Table for target practice. The restoration of the table was carried out, appropriately enough, following the restoration of the monarchy. Royalist supporters plugged the holes with wine corks and painted them over.

The forged Round Table continued to be a metaphor for the state of the monarchy itself – right down to its nineteenth-century iron rim. This device was an attempt by Queen Victoria to hold together the cracked and fragile table and it was also symbolic of the state of the crown: the table and the monarchy were both falling apart. Queen Victoria was deeply unpopular and the Republican movement was close to bringing an end to the monarchy. Just as the Round Table was being reinforced, the poet laureate Alfred Lord Tennyson published his hugely popular Arthurian epic *Idylls of the King*, a work widely credited with a massive popular revival of romantic enthusiasm for the monarchy – and support for Queen Victoria.

So much for the historical manipulation of the Round Table. What of its origins? Typically, they are obscure. The idea of the Round Table appears in literature only after the first French translators and poets in the second half of the twelfth century. At that time, it was a table that seated fifty and served to create a sense of equality among knights of various rank and influence. But it is obvious that this literary Round Table was an element from an earlier oral tradition that the French Romance poets assumed their readers were already familiar with. It is also likely that the Round Table was not entirely a literary

Knights of the Round Table – a miraculous visitation of the Holy Grail inspires and nourishes the heroic brotherhood both in body and spirit.

invention; the idea of a brotherhood of mounted knights had its historical precedents. Certainly, the historical Dux Bellorum gathered about him many independent British chieftains and although they all acknowledged Arthur as their leader in war, they addressed each other as equals. Furthermore, we know of earlier organizations of mounted warriors among the Celts that were not unlike the Round Table Knights. At the end of the second century, an independent mounted cavalry unit called the Fiana joined together to maintain and enforce a common system of justice. The real accomplishments of the Fiana lived on in the legends of the Celtic hero Finn and his noble warriors. Early Celtic bards used the cast of characters of these legends to embody particular stories that they wanted to tell. And so it is with the Arthurian tales. The Round Table is the perfect literary device: any story, character or lesson can be integrated into the Arthurian cycle so long as the story-teller invents or borrows a knight to personify it.

The tales of a vast number of knights are told within the body of Arthurian literature and many were brought to the Round Table so as to illustrate specific points. Certainly Lancelot, Perceval and Galahad were invented largely for the purpose of giving object-lessons in chivalry and to personify the Quest for the Holy Grail. Other knights were ancient Celtic heroes whose stories were older than the earliest Arthurian legends. Three of Arthur's "oldest" companions were Sir Kay, Sir Bedevere and Sir Gawain. (The shadowy Celtic deities behind these figures are the river god Kai, the one-armed war god Bedwyr and Gwalchmai, a British Hercules figure.)

Sir Gawain was one of the most active and heroic of the Round Table Knights. He was somehow able to "cross over" into the world of the righteously Christian Grail Knights while retaining his earlier, earthier personality. The tale of "Gawain and the Green Knight" is the most remarkable poem written in the English language. Beyond its artistic accomplishment, this long, anonymous, alliterative poem was used as a "text book" lesson in ideal chivalric behaviour. However, the story's resonance comes from its portrayal of Gawain as essentially good, but not tiresomely perfect.

Top Finn, the Celtic Hero – leader of the Fiana, mounted warriors and guardians of the Irish highways.
Above Sir Galahad – a knight claims his place at the Round Table.

SIR GAWAIN AND THE GREEN KNIGHT

One New Year's Eve in Camelot, the good and the great were celebrating in the court. A fire burned within the hall and all inside were in high spirits until the door burst open. With a roar and clatter of hooves, a gigantic knight mounted on a horse rode into the feasting hall. Not only was the huge knight dressed entirely in green, but his face, beard and body were a green hue, as was his mighty horse. Although of giant size, the knight was as handsome and well-proportioned as any hero. He was attired as a prince in the richest green robes trimmed in white fur. His spurs and studs were of gold, and his brooches and clasps glittered with emeralds. He wore neither helmet nor armour, but carried in one hand a branch of holly, and in the other a huge green and gold axe. So strange and miraculous was this apparition that all were silent. Holding the great axe above his head, the Green Knight bellowed a challenge to all within the great hall, daring any opponent to cut off his head on condition that, if he survived, the challenger would receive a similar stroke in a year and a day at the pilgrim site of the Green Chapel.

This was an incomprehensible challenge, but the Green Knight taunted the collected Knights of the Round Table until King Arthur himself stood to deliver the ghastly stroke. Shamed by his King's bravery, Arthur's nephew Sir Gawain begged that he might be allowed to accept the challenge. He took up the great axe and with a single blow, struck off the Green Knight's head. The whole court looked on in astonishment when the Green Knight's headless body stood up and, lifting his own severed head by the hair, mounted his green horse. Before riding off the Knight called out to Gawain to remember their bargain at the Green Chapel, and then rode away.

So, on the following All Hallows Day, Gawain set out on his pilgrimage. On Christmas Day he found he had lost his way in a forest. There he came upon a great castle where he was welcomed by a noble lord, a beautiful lady and an aged hag. The lord assured

Green Man – this legendary Celtic giant, linked to sacrificial rites of the earliest argricultural societies, found new expression in the legend of Gawain and the Green Knight.

Gawain that the chapel he sought was near at hand, and invited him to spend the intervening three days in celebration and pleasure. The two noble men then made an agreement that whatever tokens of pleasure they won during the day, in the evening each would surrender to the other. On each morning, the lord of the castle left before dawn and hunted in the woods while Gawain slept in and was awakened by the beautiful lady. She would enter his chamber and sit upon his bed, teasing the knight with obvious offers of sexual favour. Not wishing either to betray his host, or offend his hostess, Gawain carefully balanced his courtly manners and flattering banter so that he pleased the lady and yet took no improper favour. When the lord returned each night and heaped upon Sir Gawain the game he had gathered during the day, Gawain truthfully gave him tokens of whatever pleasure he had enjoyed: an innocent kiss on the first day, two on the second, and three on the third. Each time, Gawain was faithful to his host, except

Headless Horseman – the decapitated Green Knight astonishes King Arthur and the Knights of the Round Table by casually picking up his own severed head and riding away.

on the third day, when he failed to surrender a slim green silken sash embroidered with the finest gold thread that the lady had given him, claiming that it possessed the power to preserve his life and turn away the edge of any blade that might threaten him.

When Gawain arose on New Year's Day to ride to the Green Chapel, he carried with him that green silken sash out of some faint hope that it might indeed save his life. Yet that hope all but vanished when he stood before the gigantic Green Knight in the terrible Green Chapel. But Gawain kept his word; bravely bowing down, he bared his neck to the Green Knight's axe. As the axe dropped, Gawain flinched, and the Green Knight withheld the fatal stroke. And so a second time Gawain lowered his head, but slightly moved again, and the Green Knight stayed the blade. Finally, a third time Gawain held firm and cried out to the Green Knight to strike hard, which he did with great force. But that stroke delivered only a slight nick on Gawain's neck, causing but a small spurt of red blood to stain the snow.

Sir Gawain could barely believe his luck, but was greeted with the Green Knight's laughter and congratulations. For the Green Knight soon revealed that all Gawain had experienced was an illusion conjured up by Morgan Le Fay to test and shame the Knights of the Round Table. The Green Knight was the same lord who had been Gawain's host those past three days and it was he who had commanded his wife to attempt to seduce Gawain. But so good and graceful was Gawain's manner that no fault could be found, except for the one small slip of keeping the green sash. For that, the Green Knight delivered the one red nick upon Gawain's neck. Yet otherwise Sir Gawain had won the highest honour, freedom and fame.

So, Gawain, departed for Camelot, lighter of heart than when he had left the court, and there was greeted by King Arthur and Queen Guinevere. His story had preceded him and he was met with much cheer and good-hearted laughter. Thereafter, King Arthur proclaimed that all the Knights of the Round Table were required to wear a sash of green silk in honour of Gawain's quest and as a constant reminder of the knightly virtue by which men-at-arms must work to keep away all that is evil in thought and deed.

It is the humanity shown by Sir Gawain that makes this story so delightful. But there were other knights made of steelier metal. Sir Bors was one of the knights in the Quest for the Holy Grail, which was designed to bring a new puritanism to the Round Table. In this story from the *Prose Lancelot* Bors's moral strength and unwavering dedication make him far less human than Lancelot or Gawain – and far less comprehensible to us.

THE CASTLE OF MAIDENS

While Sir Bors was on his Grail Quest he found shelter one evening in the castle of a wealthy and powerful queen who was attended by a dozen lovely ladies-in-waiting. Each lady was more beautiful than the next and the queen was more beautiful than them all. Each of the ladies attempted to entice Sir Bors, but so single-minded was the knight in his dedication to his quest that they failed. The great queen herself attempted to seduce Sir Bors, but finding that this had little effect, she finally resorted to more drastic tactics. With her twelve beautiful damsels, the queen climbed the highest tower in the entire castle. There, the thirteen maidens stood in the windows of the tower ramparts and threatened to cast themselves to the ground if Sir Bors would not agree to the queen's demands.

Sir Bors proved to be a knight of steadfast – if not to say totally inflexible – principle and decided that his holy quest must take precedence over any concern for the queen and her ladies. Not for Bors the pitfalls of knights who saw their purpose only in the rescue of damsels in distress. So when he turned to ride off, the queen and all twelve maidens, shrieking horribly, furiously hurled themselves to the ground. But a moment before they struck the rocks the queen, the maidens and the castle itself all disappeared in a flash and a wisp of smoke. All that remained was a whiff of sulphur.

The Castle of Maidens – the temptation of the steadfast Sir Bors by the beautiful queen and her handmaids.

103

The tales of the Round Table Knights were intended to demonstrate all that was good in knighthood. King Arthur's knights were the embodiment of the "chivalric code" – a knightly contract of conduct in peace and war. At its best, chivalry was a genuine attempt by Christian warriors to use their privilege and power in a civilized manner, to help the downtrodden and to work toward the betterment of the human condition. However, as much as the stories of Camelot and the Round Table expressed nostalgia for the ideals of chivalry, they also painted a cautionary picture of the disastrous realities of feudalism. When Charlemagne created the Holy Roman Empire, he set up a centralized system of government and land tenure to replace Roman Imperial authority. Charlemagne's absolute temporal power was backed up by the spiritual authority (and implied divine blessing) of the Roman Church. After the break-up of the Holy Roman Empire, however, the system lost its centralizing authority and all that survived was feudalism, by which individual knights held parcels of land either by strength of arms or through the protection of a more powerful knight (to whom the "protected" knight had to swear allegiance). The result was constant war and conflict.

In Camelot's downfall we see the dramatization of the slow collapse of feudalism in Europe from 1200 to 1500. Just as the internecine warfare of feudal knights, barons, dukes and petty kings tore Europe apart in the wake of Charlemagne's rule, so was Camelot destroyed by the petty competition among the Knights of the Round Table. Even before the cataclysmic last battle of Camlann, tales were told of many Round Table Knights who were set against one another in duels and tournaments, as in this story of "The Tournament" from Malory. The result of all this in-fighting was a greatly diminished Round Table.

THE TOURNAMENT

In the wilderness far beyond the towers of Camelot, King Arthur was deceived by enchantresses and cast into a deep sleep. When he woke he found himself in a prison pit, dank and foul. Around him he could hear the creeping rats and the groans of knights who for so long had been ensnared and tortured in this vile dungeon. Eventually, the lady of the castle came to King Arthur on behalf of the lord of the castle and gave him an ultimatum: either Arthur might spend a lifetime in this pit, or he might take his chances at surviving a tournament duel to the death against another great champion. For himself alone, King Arthur replied, he would not fight. But for the sake of those others held captive in the dungeon he would gladly meet any champion. To this the lady agreed and she also offered to bring his sword Excalibur and all the armour he needed for the battle.

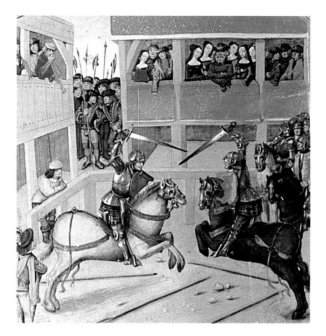

Not far from Arthur's prison pit, was another knight of the Round Table, the brave Sir Accolon of Gaul, who awoke from a spell. Soon there came to him a dwarf who brought a message from Morgan Le Fay. This lady had been Accolon's paramour and was still his lover whenever they met. "Make ready for the tournament tomorrow," said the dwarf to Accolon. "You must fight some other knight." When Accolon enquired about his opponent, the dwarf responded, "I know not who, or by what reputation, but fear not. For Morgan Le Fay has brought all her crafts and enchantments to your aid and secured for you the sword Excalibur and its scabbard. So your victory is assured."

On the next morning, both Sir Accolon and King Arthur came to the tournament field. But they knew not each other, as they entered at different ends and armed themselves in livery and armour. When King Arthur was given his sword Excalibur by the lady of the castle, he felt victory was assured. But he did not know that this was a false Excalibur forged by the sorcery of Morgan Le Fay. The true Excalibur was worn by the King's mysterious opponent. Full of confidence, King Arthur mounted his horse. So too did Sir Accolon, and both knights charged full tilt at one another. So true and steady were their lances that they struck each other's shields full on and both fell at once to earth. Yet both were soon up and with sword and shield fought now on foot. So forceful were their blows that the onlookers wondered how any might survive such battering. It was not long before Arthur was certain he had been betrayed, for each time Sir Accolon struck he drew blood from Arthur, yet when the King struck Accolon there was no blood. After a time, Arthur had shed so

Tournament – before the eyes of ladies and noblemen, King Arthur rode full tilt into that medieval form of battle that was part sport, part spectacle and part manslaughter.

105

much blood that the crowds who watched marvelled that he was not already dead. Whatever he did, Sir Accolon could not get this knight to submit, so he made up his mind to slay his brave opponent. However, in the tournament crowd was Vivien, the Lady of the Lake, who knew the sword Excalibur as she knew her own mind. She understood at once the stratagem of Morgan Le Fay.

When Arthur next battered against Accolon, Vivien cast her spell and commanded Excalibur to leap from the knight's hand and fall upon the ground. With all speed, Arthur seized the blade and knew at once that this was Excalibur. In the same instant he pushed against his foe and pulled the scabbard from his side as well. In fury at the treachery, Arthur laid about Accolon's head and body with such force that the knight was driven to his knees. But like Arthur before him, Accolon remained true to the code of the Round Table and refused to surrender. He swore he would accept death rather than submit to any other but his true king.

It was then that Arthur demanded to know the name of this knight as well as those of his king and country. Upon hearing his own name spoken and that of his own knight of Camelot, Arthur fell back in shame that he should fight a member of his own Round Table. And even Sir Accolon, who loved his mistress unto death, was filled with horror at Morgan Le Fay's treachery. The combatants then retired

Theft of Excalibur – Arthur's faery half-sister Morgan Le Fay attempted the theft of the charmed sword on many occasions, only to be foiled by its guardian, the Lady of the Lake.

106

from the field to an abbey to heal their wounds, but within a week Sir Accolon died from his wounds – another good knight ruined and the King almost slain, all by the machinations of Morgan le Fay.

It was the intrigues of the various factions of the Round Table that brought about the downfall of Camelot, and we have mourned the loss of Arthur's kingdom for over a millennium. Yet it is the destruction as much as the existence of Camelot that has made it such a potent image. Yes, the failure of Camelot signifies the ultimate triumph of evil over good, but in the Utopian ideal of Camelot mankind always sees a message of hope: what the imagination of man once built, he can build again.

So it has been through the centuries since Camelot was conceived. In the twentieth century this was most poignantly expressed by the presidency of John F. Kennedy and his "Camelot administration," which first raised and then three years later dashed the hopes of the American public. America has yet to come to terms with this tragedy. The author T.H. White has written extensively on the legends of King Arthur, and he concludes that Camelot was built on one fundamental concept: "Fight only for the good." King Arthur learned that for his day, this concept came too soon. But each succeeding generation hopes that its time will finally come again.

Camelot – a distant vision of that lost realm of King Arthur; a Utopian kingdom forever reshaped by the human imagination to fit the needs and ideals of the times.

CHAPTER ELEVEN

GUINEVERE AND LANCELOT

*As for our noble King Arthur, we love him, but as for Queen Guinevere, we
love her not because she is the destroyer of good knights.*

Le Morte d'Arthur – *Malory*

To the modern imagination, Camelot is the stage on which
the drama of one of the world's great love stories was
performed: the tragic love triangle of King Arthur, Queen
Guinevere and Sir Lancelot. Today it seems that these
star-crossed lovers must always have been an elemental part of the story of
King Arthur and Camelot, but the truth is that they appear quite late in its
evolution. It is only because the Arthurian tradition has come down to the
twentieth century largely by way of Sir Thomas Malory's fifteenth-century
epic prose masterpiece, the *Morte d'Arthur* that this love story is so central.

In Malory's "The Poisoned Apple" are dramatized all the themes that have become the
hallmarks of Arthurian Romance: passion, loyalty
and the fear of betrayal.

Below Guinevere and Lancelot –
the forbidden lovers of Camelot.
Opposite Lancelot, the Queen's
Champion – rides to her defence.

THE POISONED APPLE

In Camelot were whispered many evil rumours regarding Queen Guinevere and her champion Sir Lancelot. Chief among the conspirators was King Arthur's bastard son Sir Mordred who, well-schooled in deceit by his mother Morgan Le Fay, seldom spoke himself of Lancelot or Guinevere. Instead, he would provoke his half-brother Sir Agravain into spreading evil stories. Fearful of betrayal, Lancelot shied away from the Queen and began to spend much time with other members of the court. When Guinevere called him to her chamber and accused him of loving her no more, it did Sir Lancelot little good to speak of his fear of causing slander or shame to the Queen and the King because of their deeds. For the Queen would believe none of it, and in anger called him a liar and a lecher and claimed she would now never love him. She banished Lancelot from her court and commanded he leave at once for his own country.

So it was that the falsely accused Sir Lancelot removed himself from Camelot, much to the distress of many a knight who wished for his company, and of King Arthur himself, who was often in need of his best knight's skill and his best friend's advice. As for Queen Guinevere, she made a pretence of missing Lancelot not at all, and she now spent much time in the company of other knights of the Round Table. On one such occasion, the Queen made a feast for two dozen brave knights. Merry and long was the evening feast that Queen Guinevere prepared with her own hand. But suddenly amid the good cheer, the brave knight Sir Patrise of Ireland cried out and collapsed dead upon the table. In his hand was an apple with one bite taken from it, and in his throat was that one piece of apple that caused his throat to swell and burst. The apple had been poisoned, yet it seemed to all at the table that Sir Patrise was not the intended victim, for it was clear that the unlucky knight had taken the poisoned fruit from the plate of his comrade Sir Gawain. When Sir Mador de la Porte, the cousin of the murdered Sir Patrise, learned that it was the Queen alone who had been seen to serve up this plate of fruit, he openly accused her of murder and called out for justice.

Soon came King Arthur to the feasting hall. He heard what had befallen the knight, and how the knights all suspected the queen of the deed, but he was trapped by his duty as chief justice of the realm and could not defend his own wife. He was forced by law to grant Sir Mador a day of battle and judgment in fifteen days. On that day Guinevere must find a knight willing to prove her innocence in a trial of lance and sword. Yet, so well had worked the whispering campaign of Sir Mordred against the Queen that, with Sir Lancelot departed, no knight came forth in Guinevere's defence. Indeed, it was only through the intervention of King Arthur that Lancelot's kinsman, Sir Bors, reluctantly agreed to defend Queen Guinevere.

When the fifteenth day dawned upon the tournament field, there were raised the pavilions of the knights and ladies on one side of the meadow, and upon the other was a great pyre of wood built around an iron stake that was fired and made ready, lest Guinevere's champion lose and she be sent to the flames. So came together the two knights, although he that stood to fight Sir Mador was not at all Sir Bors. It was another knight of no known reputation who rode a white horse and carried a shield and arms that none had seen before. But since no other would stand for the Queen, the unknown knight entered the lists and against Sir Mador rode full tilt. In an instant Sir Mador's spear was shattered and both he and his horse were upon the ground. The unknown knight descended from his horse and with sword and shield the two combatants fought, neither one quite gaining the advantage. Then the unknown knight struck Sir Mador down with such force that he lay upon the ground and had his helmet ripped off. Crying out, Sir Mador surrendered, and begged for mercy.

Granted life, Sir Mador recanted his accusations, and agreed that no blame should be attributed to Queen Guinevere for the death of Sir Patrise. Thereafter, to prove the truth of this matter settled in combat, there appeared the Lady of the Lake who knew well all enchantments and sorceries. For she had come from examining the dead knight and the poisoned fruit, and she now announced to all that the evil deed had not been carried out by the Queen. Vivien revealed that the murderer was Sir Pinel le Savage who had poisoned the apple at the feast and then fled unnoticed to his own country. Sir Pinel had not wished to murder Sir Patrise, but to take the life of Sir Gawain who in time past had slain his cousin, Sir Lamorak de Gales. (Moreover, the Lady of the Lake wondered at the source of such a poison. She dared not say, but she suspected that the treachery of Sir Pinel might have been provoked by Sir Mordred, and the poison's origin might have been none other than Morgan Le Fay.)

King Arthur now thanked the unknown champion for standing up for his Queen, and for saving her that day from the cruel flames. He took up a flagon of wine and asked the knight to remove his helmet and celebrate by taking a drink with them. This the unknown knight did, and so revealed himself as Sir Lancelot.

At the sight of his best friend, King Arthur gave thanks, and so too did the Queen, who wept with love at the sight of her champion. To them Lancelot explained that he had received word from Sir Bors of the Queen's plight and rode from afar as fast as he might.

Thereafter, Sir Lancelot swore to stand ever after close to fight for his King and Queen and defend them in any quarrel. To this promise, King Arthur gave grateful thanks, although there were others who did not. This incident only helped confirm the rumours that had come before from the mouth of Sir Mordred. For there was poison working not just in the apple, but throughout the kingdom. This contest proved how few among the knighthood loved Queen Guinevere and how many would stand against her.

Defeat – Lancelot forces Sir Mador to withdraw his false accusation against Queen Guinevere.

The symbolism of a poisoned apple was frequently used in later fairy tales, most notably in "Snow White and the Seven Dwarves," and is clearly an allusion to the forbidden apple offered to Eve through which she and Adam gained carnal knowledge. The choice of a poisoned apple as the root of this Arthurian dispute thus inevitably suggests the underlying cause of discord in Camelot: the adultery of Guinevere and Lancelot. However, it also implies a comparison between Camelot and that most celebrated ancient city of Troy, whose destruction was the result of a poisonous curse placed on a golden apple, and a beautiful queen's adulterous love affair.

This great theme of "the love that destroys" was not at the core of the ancient tradition of King Arthur, but emerged over several centuries out of a series of conflicting historical traditions. In Geoffrey of Monmouth's *History of the Kings of Britain*, we are told that Arthur's wife was Queen Ganhumara, the beautiful daughter of a noble Roman family. Ganhumara's main contribution to the story is her adulterous affair with her husband's traitorous nephew Mordred. It was not until the French Romance *Lancelot* of Chretien de Troyes at the end of the twelfth century, that the name Guinevere was used. From being a peripheral figure in earlier Arthurian tradition, Guinevere was transformed into a central character. Chretien de Troyes' Queen Guinevere is a complex woman who was frequently at the centre of the

Queen Guinevere – her infidelity was gradually established as the underlying cause of discord in Camelot.

adventures of the Knights of the Round Table. As his wife grew in stature, King Arthur featured in fewer adventures and often appeared almost as a royal civil servant whose power were severely limited by the laws he was bound to enforce. How and why Queen Guinevere became more important than King Arthur is yet another example of how Camelot reflected the society that imagined it.

Starting with the mid-twelfth-century rule of the Plantagenet King Henry II and his wife Queen Eleanor of Aquitaine, the power of aristocratic women increased dramatically. The courts of Europe were run by powerful, cultured women – like the remarkable Queen Eleanor – and these women encouraged literature, music and art in their courts, as well as the romantic devotion of young knights. Indeed, the medieval court of the late twelfth and thirteenth centuries was largely a society of well-bred, well-educated women, knowledgeable in classical Greek and Latin, and filled with the medieval sense of romance. The composition of much Arthurian Romance derived directly from the patronage of Eleanor of Aquitaine, her daughters and other ladies of the court. And these women saw to it that the female Arthurian characters were major players in the works that they financed.

The literary tradition that most captivated Eleanor and her peers was that of the troubadours

Eleanor and Rosamund – Queen Eleanor was the historical model for both Guinevere and Morgan Le Fay. Here she casts a spell on Rosamund, her husband's mistress, one of many people she reputedly murdered.

of Provence in southern France. These early twelfth-century singers are credited with inventing what we know today as "romantic love," an irresistible force that refined and improved the noble lover and spurred him on to great deeds. The romantic lover was encouraged to worship his lady and in so doing, bring moral worth to his life.

The rules of ideal romantic love were formalized just as the rules of combat formalized the chivalric code, and it was through the romantic tales of the Round Table Knights that most people thrilled to accounts of chivalrous deeds and swooned at courtly love. The literature of Arthurian Romance encouraged the ideal of a new kind of knight: well-mannered, good-natured, well-spoken, educated, generous, brave, gifted as an artist and musician, courteous and above all, without equal in battle; in short, Lancelot. Just as the perils of love played an important part in the stories of chivalry and courtly romance, Sir Lancelot was the most popular of all Arthurian characters because, despite the fact that he betrayed his King by his adultery with the Queen, he did so reluctantly, driven by uncontrollable passion; and his devotion to Guinevere was complete and lifelong.

Time and again, Lancelot was the Queen's champion and saviour. The most famous of his heroic rescues of Queen Guinevere was the one that required him to cross the Sword Bridge into the shadowy Kingdom of Gorre. In Chretien de Troyes' tale we see how courtly love was a kind of dedication to Christian ideals. The extreme (one might even say masochistic) level of pain endured by Lancelot in this rescue resembles nothing so much as the sacrament of religious martyrdom.

Above **Troubadors – singers and poets who were credited with inventing the ideals of "romantic love."** *Below The Power of Lady Love* **– a fifteenth-century allegory on the power of women over men's hearts.**

LANCELOT AND THE SWORD BRIDGE

In the Kingdom of Gorre, whence no man might return, was a powerful knight called Meliagante, son to the king of that land, who so desired the Lady Guinevere that he contrived to abduct her upon a May Day festival together with many of her brave knights, who were unarmed. When Sir Lancelot learned of this, he furiously pursued the evil Meliagante to the borders of his kingdom, but found that to enter the land of Gorre he must either cross over or under a deep, swift river. He chose the most difficult route, crossing over the river by way of the Sword Bridge, a gigantic steel sword lying from bank to bank, razor-edge uppermost. Moreover, on the far bank were two chained leopards guarding the shore.

Because his lady Guinevere often claimed to doubt his dedication to her, Sir Lancelot deliberately removed the armour from his hands and feet before crawling across the cruel bridge. Terribly wounded when he reached the other side, he nevertheless attempted to fight the leopards (or in another version, a lion) guarding the far bank, only to discover that the creatures were an illusion. The King of Gorre was much impressed by this show of courage and he tried to make peace between his son and Lancelot. But Meliagante refused to relinquish Queen Guinevere, and so despite his dreadful wounds, Lancelot challenged the Prince of Gorre to fight on the following day.

The next day, the Queen's captive knights and the multitude of other folk who had been held in that land crowded around the castle square as Prince Meliagante and their champion Sir Lancelot prepared to do battle. So fiercely and hotly did the battle between the

The Rescue – Lancelot rescued Guinevere from Gorre by crossing the Sword Bridge, fighting a lion and duelling with Prince Meliagante.

two knights rage that the King at last begged Guinevere to stop them. Sir Lancelot heard her call from the window in the tower and, bowing to her command as ever, at once ceased to defend himself, even though his enemy continued to rain blows upon him. Finally the servants of the King of Gorre forced the foul Meliagante to cease his attack on the unresisting and sorely wounded Lancelot. A truce was arranged and a treaty made. Guinevere and all who were imprisoned in that land were released on the condition that Lancelot and Meliagante fight for Guinevere a year and a day later at Camelot.

Prince Meliagante attempted to gain some advantage in the intervening time by entrapping Lancelot and imprisoning him in a windowless tower. On the day of the duel Queen Guinevere was persuaded that Sir Lancelot had abandoned her for another love. But Meliagante had underestimated the ferocity of Lancelot's love: the knight escaped and appeared on the field of honour to fight for his lady. Although once again exhausted by his efforts to reach the duelling grounds, the sight of Prince Meliagante drove Sir Lancelot into a battle frenzy in which he showered vicious blows on the evil

knight. Meliagante was driven to the ground and slain and thus Sir Lancelot proved himself a true and faithful knight and Guinevere's freedom and honour were restored.

The character of Queen Guinevere evolved in a curious manner after the early French Romances such as those of Chretien de Troyes. Within a century, the clergy took these popular tales and edited them to suit their own didactic purposes. The most monumental of these undertakings was that of the *Prose Lancelot*, also known as *The Vulgate Cycle*, which was compiled by the scribes of the Cistercian monastic order (the same Cistercian monks whose anti-female bias resulted in the demonization of Morgan Le Fay). Consequently, the flirtatious and whimsical Queen Guinevere became a petulant destroyer of knights and a betrayer of her king and country. The Cistercian scribes also transformed the character of Lancelot from a peerless warrior into a tortured adulterer whose sin prevented him from attaining the Holy Grail.

Lancelot's origins predate Camelot and it is likely that they spring from the Irish warrior god Lugh Lamhfada and the Welsh warrior hero Lluch Llauynnauc. But according to the early

Left Romantic Lovers – transformed by Cistercian scribes into guilty sinners destroyed by their moral lapse. *Opposite* Penitence – in remorse for her adultery, Guinevere locked herself away in a convent.

Arthurian legends, Lancelot was the son of Ban of Benoic, a king of Brittany slain in battle. After his father's death the newborn Lancelot was stolen away by the Lady of the Lake and fostered in her underwater realm. Raised by water nymphs, Lancelot emerged at fifteen as the ultimate knight in war and in peace. He was given shining armour and weapons by the Lady of the Lake and was sent to King Arthur's court. There he became Queen Guinevere's champion and often fought for the good and honour of all the Knights of the Round Table. In time, he had two love affairs and eventually happily married a faithful wife. In these versions of Lancelot's life there was no implication of adultery with the Queen.

By the time Chretien de Troyes wrote his French Romance *Lancelot* in 1172, the hero had become the prototypical chivalrous knight and courtly lover. According to Chretien, Lancelot's union with Queen Guinevere is bliss and joy and occasions not a hint of remorse. However, when the Cistercian scribes rewrote the Arthurian tales in the *Prose Lancelot* some sixty years later, they highjacked the character of this good knight to convey their own moral agenda. Lancelot and Guinevere are now given a monumental sense of guilt and a crushing punishment for their adultery. There is not even a fleeting moment of joy for them. Immediately after the act, Lancelot is bleating "It would be better for me that I had never been born." Never one for doing anything by halves, Lancelot then dons a hair shirt and becomes a self-flagellating hermit tormented by his terrible sin.

A powerful influence on the character of Queen Guinevere was the legend of Tristan and Iseult (Tristram and Isolde), an early version of which

was written by Marie de France, a possibly illegitimate daughter of Henry II. In this triangular love story, itself based on the Greek legend of Theseus and Ariadne, Tristan, the nephew of King Mark of Cornwall, wins the Princess Iseult for his uncle. However, before the two can marry, Tristan and Iseult accidentally drink a wine-potion and fall in love. Nevertheless, the marriage between Iseult and Mark goes ahead, while the lovesick Tristan marries someone else, another Iseult, this time of Brittany. When Tristan hears a false report of his first love's death, he dies of a broken heart, soon followed by the grief-stricken Iseult of Cornwall.

Clearly, there are many parallels here with the doomed love triangle of Lancelot, Arthur and Guinevere. In both tales, we have the moral crisis of divided loyalties, the clash of love and duty, passion and intelligence.

One further influence in the shaping of the Lancelot and Guinevere tale was undoubtedly the famous twelfth-century true story of Abelard and Heloise. Peter Abelard was the most renowned French philosopher and theologian of his time and when he was forty years old, he fell in love with a student named Heloise, with whom he had a child. Heloise's uncle, a canon at Notre Dame, was outraged, and had Abelard castrated. Abelard then took orders in the monastery at St. Denis and Heloise joined a convent and became a nun. However, their love survived even this setback and their physical passion transcended to a spiritual plane. Their letters were as intense on spiritual matters as

Tristram and Isolde – tragic medieval lovers whose passion violated the vows of marriage. Like Lancelot and Guinevere, they came to a disastrous end, but the legend of their love became immortal.

they had once been on sensual matters. Abelard addressed his letters regularly to Heloise, "once my wife and now my sister in Christ." This was too much for many clerics of the day. Not only did Abelard appear to take this woman's opinions seriously, the whole relationship smacked of courtly love. One of those who viewed Abelard's influence as corrupting was Bernard of Clairvaux – the philosopher and founder of the Cistercian order – who obviously felt castration and a lifetime of celibacy were not sufficient deterrents to temptations of the flesh. So Bernard campaigned for Abelard's conviction for heresy and his excommunication from the church. In this he succeeded and thereafter, it was Bernard of Clairvaux who rose to the position of the most famous theologian of his day.

Indeed, the *Prose Lancelot* portrayal of Lancelot as the ultimate reformed sinner is straight out of Bernard's text on the subject, *The Steps of Humility*. The valiant – if obsessive – Lancelot followed St Bernard's road to salvation to the letter: he rejected mortal temptations and ambition; he withdrew from the world and the flesh, and through austerity and mortification the penitent sinner found salvation and mystical union with God. But if the Cistercians made Lancelot their moral whipping boy, they also needed him to fulfil the prophecy by which he would father Galahad, the knight destined to achieve the Holy Grail. In Malory's story of "Lancelot and Elaine," Lancelot is tricked into siring Galahad in much the same way as Merlin tricked Igraine into inviting Uther Pendragon into her bed, an invitation that resulted in the conception of Arthur.

LANCELOT AND ELAINE

The realm of King Pelles was under the enchantment of an evil serpent and, furthermore, Queen Morgan le Fay and the Queen of the Northgales had locked the King's daughter Elaine in a great tower because her beauty was said to exceed theirs. The tower burned with the heat of a furnace and the maid was forced to walk around naked as a needle. Now, when the noble Sir Lancelot came to the haunted kingdom, all the people rejoiced for they knew that he would be their saviour. Lancelot climbed the hellish tower, rescued the princess, clothed her and took her to the safety of the chapel. Yet at the chapel a second challenge awaited them: a serpent lying beneath a tomb. Lancelot used his strength to lift the stone and then bravely

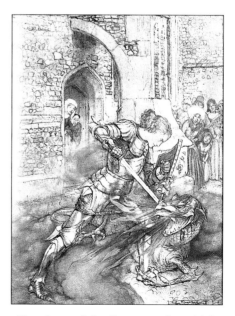

Slaughter of the Serpent – by which Lancelot lifted the curse of Morgan Le Fay from the realm of King Pelles and his captive daughter, Elaine.

fought the fire-breathing serpent and slew him. It was by this deed
that Lancelot saved the realm of King Pelles. For a time the great
knight remained in that place, much beloved by its people and by the
King, who knew a prophecy which foretold that his daughter Elaine
was destined to give birth to Lancelot's child, Galahad. And so, by
order of the King, Lancelot was deceived by that realm's chief
enchantress, Dame Brisen into lying with Elaine, believing her to be
his beautiful Guinevere. In this way did Lancelot and Elaine beget that
child of destiny, Galahad, the perfect knight.

According to Malory, another Elaine who failed to take Guinevere's place
in Lancelot's affections was the Lady of Astolat, immortalized in Tennyson's
poem as the Lady of Shalott. Elaine of Astolat asked Lancelot to wear her
sleeve as a token when he took part in a tournament and although Lancelot
never wore a lady's token, he agreed to Elaine's request on this occasion as
he did not want to be recognized. The ruse worked, but he was gravely
wounded, unwittingly, by Sir Bors. It was the Lady of Astolat who nursed
Lancelot back to health, and she came to love him "with that love that was
her doom." However, he had no desire to be her husband or her paramour,
and at his rejection she died of heartbreak, asking
that her body be borne down the river on a

**Lady of Shalott – Elaine's unrequited
love for Lancelot was so strong that
she died of a broken heart.**

barge. When her body floated by Camelot, King Arthur decreed that she be buried like a queen, and on her tomb was written her sad story.

Guinevere and Lancelot were destined to be the great loves of each other's lives. But they were not destined to live happily ever after; the Cistercians saw to that. According to the *Prose Lancelot*, after their union, the Queen falls to predicting the disastrous consequences of their actions: the destruction of Camelot, the death of nearly all the noblest knights in the world, the death of the greatest king and the damnation of their own souls. "Through thee and me is the flower of kings and knights destroyed," says Guinevere. Then she begs: "Sir Lancelot, I ask thee, for all the love that ever was betwixt us, that thou never see me more." The lovers part for the rest of their tortured lives. Guinevere goes to a convent and Lancelot to a hermitage. After years of self-abasement Lancelot is summoned by a dream in which he sees Guinevere dying. It is a truthful vision, for Guinevere has passed away with these, her last words: "I beseech Almighty God that I may never have power to see Lancelot with my worldly eyes." With the release of Guinevere's soul, Lancelot lets go of his final tie to the mortal world. He stretches out upon Guinevere's tomb, and finally earns his true salvation. His soul is lifted up to the heavens by a host of angels.

Out of a complex jumble of history, theology, philosophy, high romance and human tragedy, one of the great love stories of our heritage took shape and found its place within the realm of Camelot. The story of Lancelot and Guinevere has played its part in shaping our own ideas of romantic love as have only a handful of others. In their story we celebrate both the sacred and profane natures of romantic love, a dangerous passion that is beyond control or reason.

Guinevere's Funeral – attended by the convent nuns and the grief-stricken Lancelot, dressed in the white robes of a Cistercian monk.

CHAPTER TWELVE

THE QUEST OF THE HOLY GRAIL

With the Quest of Sangrail all you of the Round Table shall depart,
and never shall I see you wholly together again.
Le Morte d'Arthur – *Malory*

In Arthurian Romance one great quest took precedence over all others: the Quest of the Holy Grail. Tales of the Grail Quest reached the height of their popularity during the holy wars of the Crusades. This was no accident, for both endeavours might be described – depending on your point of view – as either inspired or mad. In both cases, there is little doubt of the disastrous consequences for both the fictional and the historical knights involved.

The Holy Grail itself was different things at different times – a platter, cup, cauldron, stone, dish, chalice or horn of plenty – but by the thirteenth century its pedigree was broadly established. Of the many tales of its origin, there were two that formed the basis of popular belief and firmly established a connection between the Arthurian knighthood and Jesus Christ. The following, earlier version by Robert de Boron introduces the character of the Fisher King, also known as King Bron, who was clearly derived from Bran, the Celtic god identified with the salmon.

The Holy Grail – variously described as a platter, cauldron, stone, dish, chalice and horn of plenty.

THE HOLY GRAIL AND
THE FISHER KING

While Christ suffered on the Cross, Joseph of Arimathea used the Grail to catch His blood. He then buried the body of Christ and was for this reason himself sealed up alive in a tomb by the Jews. After many years had passed, the emperor Vespasian went to Jerusalem and had the bricked-up tomb opened. Miraculously, Joseph of Arimathea was still alive, for the Holy Grail had fed and nourished him for all the years of his entombment. The Emperor granted Joseph's freedom and together with his sister Enygeus, he travelled far away from Judea. With Enygeus's husband King Bron, the siblings formed a thriving community, but after a time the sins of its members caused the crops to fail. Joseph instructed the people to build a round table which was a replica of the table used at the Last Supper. Upon that table would be placed the Holy Grail and a fish caught by King Bron. Only those whose souls were pure could bear to sit at the round table in the presence of the Holy Grail, for by the power of the Grail were they nourished with the body of the fish and filled with a sacred bliss that flowed from the blood of Christ held within the Holy Grail.

The Grail Maiden – carrying aloft the radiant Holy Grail, the legendary vessel used by Joseph of Arimathea to catch the blood of Christ.

When this purification ritual was completed, the land and crops were indeed restored to fertility. King Bron and Enygeus had twelve sons, one of whom, Alain, chose the sacred life and celibacy. Nonetheless, Joseph of Arimathea recognized that it was Alain who was destined to become the father of the Grail Knight. So Joseph taught him the secrets of the Grail and when his life drew to a close, Joseph gave the Holy Grail to Alain. This new guardian of the Holy Grail took it up into the west of Britain. There he formed a new community, and a castle wherein the Holy Grail was kept.

This second account from the *Prose Lancelot* identifies the location of the Grail as Corbenic Castle, a name that – as we shall learn – signified not only the origins of the Christian Grail, but also the ancient pagan origins of the legend.

THE HOLY GRAIL AND THE CASTLE CORBENIC

It was Joseph of Arimathea who collected the blood of the crucified Christ in a dish used during the Last Supper. He and his son Josephus kept the Grail and its sacred contents hidden for many years until one day they set out on a divinely inspired journey across the world in search of a safe refuge where the holy relic might be kept. During their pilgrimage Joseph converted the pagan kings Seraphe and Evallach, who took the Christian names Mordrain and Nascien. To these two kings Joseph of Arimathea prophesied the future of the Holy Grail and the line of kings who would be its protectors. Finally, Joseph and Josephus with the kings Mordrain and Nascien and their followers came to the shores of Britain.

Josephus Holding Mass for his Followers – by the power of the Holy Grail he summons the presence of Jesus Christ and His Angels.

There they found their chosen land and established a holy community. After the death of Joseph of Arimathea and his son Josephus, their descendants and disciples built a castle called Corbenic to house the sacred vessel of the Holy Grail. In time there arose disputes among the community. King Mordrain was blinded by divine light when he came too close to the Holy Grail, and the land around the Grail Castle was cursed by a spell that rendered it barren and sterile. These hard times had been foretold by Joseph of Arimathea before he had even arrived in Britain. But Joseph had further prophesied that one day to Corbenic would come the Good Knight who would be their saviour and lift the curse of the spell. He would cure the King Mordrain of his blindness, and restore fertility to the land.

It was a combination of these two versions – and many others – that came to be popularly understood as the history of the Holy Grail. However, elements of the Grail Quest were apparent in the earliest Celtic tales, many of which involved quests for magic cauldrons. One of the older Celtic myths associated with King Arthur was of this sort. In the ancient cryptic Welsh poem *The Treasures of Britain* – probably the earliest-known example of the Grail Quest – a Dark Age King Arthur sailed with a band of heroes in a great ship to the land of Annwn. There they discovered a massive glass castle magically revolving in an isle ringed by the blue sea. At the castle's centre was the object of the quest, the pearl-rimmed cauldron of plenty that was also a cauldron of prophecy and inspiration kindled by the breath of nine maidens. Arthur and the heroes of Britain attempted to carry off the cauldron, but the perils proved overwhelming. The mission failed, and of all those who set out, only seven returned to Britain.

Quest-cauldrons took many forms, but all were imbued with similar magical qualities: they provided nourishment and, in bringing forth life, fruitfulness. In Greek mythology, the shape of the cauldron was sometimes formalized in the Cornucopia or the Horn of Plenty and was usually associated with the worship of the goddess of crops, Demeter. Linguistically there is a curious connection between the ancient Greek (and later Celtic) concept of the pagan Horn of Plenty and the Christian Holy Grail: the Grail Castle was traditionally known as "Corbenic." The name comes from the Welsh word *cors* meaning "horn", which was confused with the French *corps* meaning "body."

The Holy Grail – often represented as a chalice, but in its earliest Celtic forms it was a magic cauldron: the source of nourishment, inspiration, eternal life or infinite wealth.

Consequently, the legendary Celtic "Corbenic" meaning "Castle of the "Blessed Horn (of Plenty)" was translated by the French Romance poets as "Corbenoit" to mean "Castle of the Blessed Body (of Christ)," as signified by its possession of the Holy Grail which contained the blood of Christ.

The quest for a magical cauldron was also an aspect of the ancient Irish legend of the Dagda, a god-like giant. The Dagda's cauldron provided a never-ending supply of nourishment in both the physical and spiritual sense. Both the Irish tales of Bran the Blessed (another variation of Bran the Salmon God) and Cuchulainn (the Irish Hercules) featured cauldrons that possessed the ability to bring the dead back to life. Indeed, the cauldron and the Cornucopia are both symbols of fertility rituals and the rites of spring which were common to nearly all early

Arthur Gazes into the Cauldron of Prophecy – and discovers it also has the power to restore life to warriors slain in battle.

agricultural societies. These pagan symbols were at first only thinly disguised by Christian dogma in the tales of the Holy Grail. In later stories, however, the Castle of the Holy Grail became allegorically Christian and was increasingly attended by angels and all manner of marvellous spirits. The Grail itself became specifically a Christian relic which was always associated with the blood of Christ, but which could take on a variety of forms. In one of the most elaborate and striking of the Grail Romances, the German *Parzival,* composed in 1205 by Wolfram von Eschenbach, the Grail is a magical stone. In his epilogue, Wolfram gives some clues to his own sources of the Grail legend when he criticizes the French Romance poets for misrepresenting what he considers the source of the story: an Arabic manuscript brought from the Holy Land by Crusader knights. In fact, there is some credence to this, for there are Oriental aspects to the Grail Quest, and among those who embraced it most enthusiastically were the military brotherhood of the Crusader Templar Knights.

Although they were not themselves questing for the Grail, during the Crusades of the thirteenth century, the Templar Knights were engaged in an equally questionable campaign: the recovery of a piece of the "True Cross" from the Holy Land – a medieval fake which the Saracens eventually surrendered to them. The Templars saw themselves as knights in search of the Grail and their order consciously forged links with the legends of the Quest of the Holy Grail. Not only did they adapt aspects of the Grail Quest to suit their own rituals, but they actually wrote or rewrote the Grail legends to mirror and advocate the ideals of the Templar Knighthood.

The Templar Knights were the militant arm of the Cistercian Order of monks, the same Cistercians who blackened the character of Morgan Le Fay and transformed Sir Lancelot into a guilt-ridden penitent. However, these adjustments to Arthurian legends were minor compared to the extensive work they did on the Quest of the Holy Grail, which they transformed into a didactic allegory on the Christian doctrine of grace and salvation according to the teachings of the Cistercian philospher Bernard of Clairvaux, and they aggressively employed the Grail Quest legend as a vehicle to advance the ideals of Templar Knighthood. The Templars emphasized (or perhaps invented) the idea that the Last Supper was served on a round table presided over by Christ.

Galahad and his Angel – in search of the Holy Grail. As Lancelot's son, Galahad was equal to his father in courage and wisdom. However, he succeeded where his father failed because he was without sin.

This implied that both King Arthur's Round Table Knights and latter-day Christian knights (including the Templar Knights) had an obligation to become warrior disciples of Christ whose duty was not to any nation or earthly king, but to the Christian faith and to God.

In the tale of the "Quest of the Holy Grail" as it has come down to us from the *Prose Lancelot*, it is reasonably easy to discern the elements that served as didactic lessons for Templar initiates. The three major figures in the Grail Quest embody fairly explicitly the ideals of the Templar Knights: valour, wisdom and virtue. But of the three knights who succeed in entering the Grail Castle – Perceval, Lancelot and Galahad – it is only Galahad who succeeds in the quest.

THE QUEST OF THE HOLY GRAIL

Merlin came to Camelot to advise King Arthur of a means of drawing together all the knights of the realm. Forming a brotherhood of knights assembled about a great round table would "show that none have precedence over any other." In the midst of the great hall, Merlin made appear that Table with 150 seats, each bearing the name of the knight destined to sit there. But the seat to the right of King Arthur, known as the "Siege Perilous," was to remain empty "in memory of Our Lord Jesus Christ," and none might sit there without penalty of instant death unless he was truly "the best knight in the world who will find the Holy Grail and know its truth and its meaning."

After many years of adventures, on the day of the Pentecost, there appeared on the Siege Perilous in golden letters "On this day, this seat will know its master." And on that day there appeared floating down the river a great stone of red marble with a marvellous sword thrust in it. The stone was carried before the King and the Knights of the Round Table, for it bore an inscription that the sword could be removed only by the best knight in the world. Lancelot refused the challenge; Gawain reluctantly tried but failed. All was silent until a wise man appeared with a young man, unknown to the others. When the golden-haired youth entered the hall, all the windows and doors closed of their own accord. The young man readily seized the sword and drew it easily from the stone. This young hero was Galahad, and was now recognized as Lancelot's son. In celebration, Galahad took his place unscathed in the Siege Perilous next to the King. Miraculously, the Holy Grail appeared (though hidden behind a veil) and gave up food and drink for all seated at the table, before vanishing suddenly.

The appearance of Galahad and the Grail provoked much debate among the

Miracle of the Floating Stone – a block of red marble in which was thrust a marvellous sword that no knight save Galahad could draw.

Knights of the Round Table. In the end, much to King Arthur's grief, the Knights swore to find the Grail Castle and discover its secrets and wonders. But the Castle was so elusive that it was capable of vanishing and moving with a will of its own. None could be guided to it, nor could it be found on any map. Thus, although many knights went out into the wilderness looking for the Grail Castle, only three succeeded in entering the castle and gazing upon the wonder of the Holy Grail.

The first to discover the Grail Castle was one of the best but least experienced of King Arthur's knights. The young and naive Sir Perceval was courageous and virtuous, but he knew nothing of the proper conventions a knight should observe while a guest in this strange castle. Perceval was brought to the feasting hall where sat a brotherhood of knights around the maimed Fisher King, who was suffering from a terrible wound that would not heal. Secretly wishing he might ask if he could do something to relieve the king's suffering, Perceval nevertheless refrained from speaking because he believed it improper to question his host. Then came a wonderful procession led by a beautiful maiden bearing the glowing, jewelled Grail. The Grail's radiant presence nourished all within the great hall with a sumptuous feast. Perceval was amazed, but nevertheless held his tongue and did not comment on the Grail's astonishing performance. After spending a night in the castle, he awoke to find it entirely deserted. In the court-yard he mounted his horse and rode over the drawbridge which was raised behind him. Then, the castle vanished entirely from sight.

When he returned to Camelot, Perceval learned that he could have achieved the Quest of the Grail if he had only spoken words that matched his thoughts. He failed in three ways: first, he asked nothing of the Fisher King, nor showed any sympathy or concern for the King's suffering as any Christian might for Christ's suffering. Secondly, he asked nothing of the Grail Maiden, nor the meaning or purpose of the Grail procession. Thirdly, he asked no one about the miracle of the Grail, nor did he show awe and wonder while in the presence of its mystery. In fact, the mysterious castle was Perceval's birthright, but

Sir Perceval – he failed to ask three vital questions about the Fisher King's suffering, the maiden's procession and the Grail's mystery.

because of his ignorance, he had caused the Fisher King unnecessary pain. Henceforth, the realm of the Fisher King was to be a waste-land of famine, drought and despair.

The next to come within sight of the Grail Castle was Sir Lancelot. Lancelot realized that he could not reach the Grail Castle by physical effort or by force of arms. This was a spiritual quest and so he knew he must seek the Grail through a spiritual journey: he became a devout hermit who wandered the wilderness, fasting and praying. So great was Lancelot's effort and dedication, that one night there appeared to him a ghostly ship sailing by moonlight without captain or crew. Lancelot boarded the vessel, and soon found he had been taken across the waters to a rocky cliff on which stood the long-sought Castle of the Holy Grail. Out of the darkness a voice beckoned. At the entrance to the castle were two fierce lions. When Lancelot tried to draw his sword, the voice bade him walk forward in peace and he

went unmolested by the guardian beasts. Within the castle Lancelot heard a voice of unearthly beauty singing. Then a door to a chapel was opened to reveal a brilliant light. He was commanded not to enter the holy place, being tainted with the sin of his adultery with Guinevere, but because of his courageous spirit he was permitted at least to see the holy object from a distance. Within the chapel Lancelot could make out the brilliantly glowing Grail on a table of silver. It was covered with a cloth of red samite, and winged angels hovered about a mysterious angelic priest who celebrated high mass. This was the magnificent vision granted the hero. However, so great was Lancelot's yearning for the Holy Grail that he stepped forward. He was instantly struck down by a cruel blast of fire and lay for twenty-four days in a death-like coma before he was able to rise again and take his leave forever from the Grail Castle.

In the end, it was Lancelot's son, the "purest" knight of the brotherhood who achieved the Grail Quest. This was Sir Galahad, the Red Cross Knight, who was of such stainless character and was so filled with Christian

The Red Cross Knight, Galahad – finally allowed to gaze upon the supreme mystery of Holy Grail.

goodness that sin could find no place in him to thrive. After many adventures and perils, Sir Galahad came at last to the Grail Castle. By his goodness, his wisdom and his courage, he entered the sacred chapel and was permitted to kneel before the Holy Grail and pray for the pain of the maimed Fisher King to cease. At once the King's wounds were healed, and his barren kingdom became green and fruitful again. However, when the last mantle of samite was drawn back from the Chalice of the Holy Grail and Galahad was permitted to gaze fully into the indescribable mystery, the knight found he had no desire to remain within this world. Increasingly filled with the wonder of the miracle, Galahad became more and more a spiritual being, until at last his body was borne aloft by angels to the gates of paradise. And with that perfect knight, the Holy Grail ascended to heaven as well.

In the tale of the Grail Quest we can see an expression of the philosophy and ideals of the Templar Knights. Perceval was a knight of great natural bravery and virtue but, just as a pagan – however good and worthy – could never enter heaven without learning the teachings of Christ, so Perceval could not attain the Grail without

Tapestry of the Grail Quest – showing four of the stages in Sir Galahad's attainment of the Holy Grail.

wisdom. Sir Lancelot was a knight supremely educated in the chivalric tradition and was more courageous than any man on earth. But Lancelot lacked moral strength and his sin of adultery prevented him from winning the Grail. It was only Sir Galahad who possessed the triple gifts of valour, wisdom and virtue who was deemed worthy of attaining the Grail.

The Quest of the Holy Grail was a glorious and inspired adventure, but even for that most perfect of knights, Sir Galahad, it was impossibly idealistic and other-worldly. To some extent, this proved true of the mission of the Templar Knights as well. With some justification, the French kings feared this powerful and secretive knighthood of zealots who believed they owed fealty to no earthly king. Certainly, their power and influence were a threat to the authority of the monarchy and eventually, King Philip the Fair decided he would tolerate them no more. Accordingly, in 1307 he abolished the Order of the Templar Knights. He had the Grand Master of the Order, Jacques de Molay tortured and burned for crimes of satanism and outrageous sexual practices. The remaining Templars were hunted, and burned as heretics and all their wealth and property were seized by the crown. And so the other-worldly ideals of the Grail Quest ultimately proved as disastrous for the historical Templar Knights as they did for the fictional knights of King Arthur's Round Table.

CHAPTER THIRTEEN

THE LAST BATTLE

Never since was there seen a more doleful battle in Christian Lands.
Le Morte d'Arthur - *Malory*

The Quest of the Holy Grail broke apart the mighty alliance of the Round Table, as King Arthur had feared it would. Many of his bravest knights had given their lives for the Quest and now that the Grail had been achieved, the surviving knights could find no great new purpose; all worldly deeds seemed soulless and empty. Then, too, Merlin was gone, forever entrapped by the enchantments of the Lady of the Lake. There were disputes between the knights, and King Arthur's authority was constantly undermined by Queen Guinevere's infidelity with his greatest knight, Sir Lancelot.

Behind all this turmoil and discord was the fatal hand of Morgan Le Fay. Her ancient curse against her brother and his earthly kingdom neared its fulfilment. That curse was manifest in Morgan's bastard son, the dark knight Sir Mordred, the unholy offspring of her incestuous and adulterous union with Arthur. Mordred was raised secretly by Morgan and trained in the arts of war and black magic. Upon maturity, he rode to Camelot and declared his heritage to all. Then, hiding his wrath, Mordred falsely proclaimed his love and loyalty to his father, King Arthur. The King generously welcomed Mordred to Camelot, and honoured him by giving him a place at the Round Table. This proved a fatal error, for Mordred (with Morgan's help) conspired within the ranks of the Knights of the Round Table, and plotted to overthrow King Arthur and seize the throne.

THE LAST DAYS OF KING ARTHUR

Sir Mordred had infected the court of Camelot with the notion that Queen Guinevere and Lancelot were betraying the King in an adulterous affair. Now he decided to make his move. With his kin Sir Aggravain, Mordred confronted the King and offered to catch the lovers in a tryst. So perilous had King Arthur's position become that he could do nothing but permit the entrapment and pray that the lovers not get caught.

Arthur Challenges Mordred – the last enemy on the field – although Bedevere begs him not to fight on.

Unfortunately, Mordred found Lancelot in Guinevere's chamber, and the Queen was condemned to death by burning. Still, King Arthur had one last hope, for he was certain that Sir Lancelot would never allow Queen Guinevere to suffer such a fate. And indeed on the day of execution, Lancelot swept all aside and rescued Queen Guinevere from the pyre. But in the ensuing battle, Lancelot unwittingly slew two young knights, who turned out to be brothers of Sir Gawain. This proved to be disastrous. The already divided loyalties of the Round Table erupted and Camelot was catapulted into civil war. Lancelot and his allies retreated to his Castle of Joyous Garde where they were followed by the armies of Sir Gawain and King Arthur. There ensued a long and bloody siege and it took the intervention of the Pope to end the conflict by banishing Lancelot to France. But the strife did not end there, for Gawain was committed with all his being to exacting revenge for his brothers' deaths, and the reluctant King Arthur had no choice but to follow Gawain to France. Finally, Gawain found Lancelot and forced the reluctant knight to fight a duel. After many fierce hours, the duel ended with Lancelot's tearful refusal to kill the badly wounded Sir Gawain. Worse still, news soon reached King Arthur that back in England, the evil Sir Mordred had seized both Arthur's crown and Queen Guinevere.

With his sadly depleted forces, King Arthur returned from France and mounted a

Above and *below* Sir Lancelot with his Allies – together they defy the law of the land and ride to rescue Queen Guinevere from the executioner's flames.

campaign against Mordred, and it was during one of these battles that Sir Gawain died of the wound sustained in his duel with Lancelot. With his dying breath Gawain voiced his regret that his lust for vengeance would inevitably bring about Camelot's destruction. The armies of Arthur and Mordred finally met on Salisbury Plain near the ancient monument of Stonehenge. On that field of slaughter, all the knights on either side were slain, except one, Sir Bedevere. It was he who attended the terribly wounded King Arthur among the heaped corpses. For only Sir Bedevere had witnessed the last fatal duel under the darkening sky between King Arthur and Sir Mordred. Bedevere saw Arthur run straight at his enemy. He watched as the King drove his long spear through Mordred's breast, but saw how the dying Mordred struck fiercely with his sword. This stroke sheared through King Arthur's helmet and delivered his fatal wound.

This was the last battle of King Arthur's knights – and the eclipse of his kingdom – as imagined by Thomas Malory in that greatest of all English Arthurian epics the *Morte d'Arthur*. Written and published at the end of the fifteenth century, Malory's last battle is very much a fifteenth-century conflict fought with weapons and armour of that period. But what of the historical Arthur's final conflict in the sixth century? The location of this battle is a matter of some dispute (possibilities include Camel Bridge on the Camel River in Cornwall, Queen Camel on the River Cam near Cadbury Castle, Camlan in North Wales, and – perhaps most likely – Camboglanna on Hadrian's Wall) but what is not disputed is Arthur's connection with this battle. The Welsh chronicle known as the *Annales Cambriae* (compiled in AD 956) notes the only major events of 539: "Battle of Camlann in which Arthur and Medraut are slain, and there are many deaths (by plague) throughout Britain and Ireland." We learn nothing more, nor are we told whether Arthur and Medraut are enemies or comrades-in-arms. What this brief record does tell us is that in the tenth century the Battle of Camlann was so famous and the story of Arthur and Medraut so well-known that they needed no explanation. From those ancient poems, the Welsh Triads, we can piece together a version of Arthur's last battle that is rather different from Malory's.

The Final Duel – Arthur and Mordred clash upon the field of slaughter that saw the obliteration of both armies.

THE BATTLE OF CAMLANN

Once, while Arthur had gone adventuring, another powerful warlord named Medraut led his forces into Arthur's realm. He pillaged Arthur's lands and robbed his fortress. Then Medraut humiliated Queen Gwenhwyfar by dragging her from the throne and ravaging her. When the furious Arthur returned, he burnt and pillaged Medraut's kingdom. But Medraut himself had fled and could not be discovered by the vengeful Arthur. Some time later, Arthur went off again to war in Brittany. There the King had one victory after another but in winning all his battles, he lost the best of his knights. When spies brought news of Arthur's weakened army, Medraut made his move. He seized Arthur's throne and abducted Queen Gwenhwyfar. Then Medraut made an unholy alliance with the pagan Picts, Scots and Saxons to create an army of such size and ferocity that he believed Arthur would not dare return. But Medraut was wrong to doubt

Death – Mordred is impaled upon Arthur's lance, but in dying, his sword delivers the king a mortal wound.

Arthur's courage, and the fearless warrior invaded and marched on Medraut's forces. At the terrible Battle of Camlann all of Medraut's men perished, while of Arthur's tribe, only three lived beyond that day. Among the scattered and stacked bodies of annihilated knights,

Medraut and Arthur searched until they discovered one another. Then these two grim warriors fought one last duel. Arthur slew Medraut, but in so doing received his own mortal wound.

By the time *The History of the Kings of Britain* was written by Geoffrey of Monmouth in 1136, Medraut had become Mordred. This Mordred was King Arthur's nephew by way of his sister, Anna. However, there was nothing incestuous or illegitimate about his birth: Mordred was the second son of Anna's husband, King Lot of Lodonesia. According to Geoffrey, the destruction of Arthur's realm came about because King Arthur foolishly entrusted Mordred and Queen Guinevere with the regency while he went off to fight foreign wars in Gaul. Geoffrey tells a fascinating story in which the consequences of the Battle of Camlann are prefigured in Arthur's dream, but are misinterpreted – with disastrous consequences – by the king's advisers.

THE DRAGON AND THE BEAR

After years of relative peace in Camelot, Arthur heard one day that the emperor Leo had summoned the Imperial army of Romans and all the kings of the Orient to make war on the Britons. So Arthur called up an army of Britons and all the kings of the North to meet this challenge. Although Arthur's army was by far the smaller of the two, he chose to fight the Imperial forces in the land of his enemies in Gaul. Upon departing, he set up a government to rule and defend Britain in his absence, leaving the governing of the land to his queen Guinevere and his nephew Mordred. Arthur then set off across the channel with joy in his heart. Yet, upon the sea, he fell into a deep slumber and dreamed a terrible dream. In this dream, he saw a Bear flying through the night sky. The huge growling Bear made every shore quake. Then out of the western sky came a winged Dragon roaring and illuminating the whole countryside with the lightning glare of its eyes. In the midst of the sky, these two monsters collided and the debacle began.

To Avalon – the world-weary King Arthur sails to Avalon in the hope that Morgan and her hand-maidens might heal his dreadful, mortal wounds.

The cataclysm shook the earth, but the Dragon gained the upper hand. Again and again he attacked the Bear, burning it with his fiery breath and finally hurling it from the sky.

So shaken was Arthur by this dream that he called his wizards to him to tell him its meaning. They declared that the conflict of the two celestial monsters foretold the outcome of a great battle the King would soon fight. In their reading of the dream, they saw the Dragon as Arthur and the Bear as his enemy, but what enemy? They prophesied it was some terrible giant that Arthur alone would fight and overcome in battle. But Arthur felt that such an enemy was too small an opponent for such a prophetic dream. He himself ventured to interpret it in such a way as to see the Bear as his greatest enemy, Emperor Leo. In any event, Arthur and his army continued on their journey to Gaul, never suspecting that what had been set in motion would bring ruin to Camelot.

In Geoffrey's *History of the Kings of Britain* Arthur's subsequent victory over the Emperor's forces is portrayed as Pyrrhic at best. Although he technically defeated the Imperial army, he destroyed the better part of his troops, along with the cream of his knighthood. As he marched toward Rome in the hope of seizing the Imperial crown, Arthur received the news that his nephew Mordred had revolted and taken Guinevere as his Queen. Mordred had also made an alliance with the Picts and the Saxons, and had assembled a vast occupying army. Yet, when Arthur returned from Gaul with an army of Breton knights, he drove Mordred's armies across Britain in a series of bloody battles. Finally, all of Mordred's forces and all those of Arthur confronted each other on the banks of the River Camblam in Cornwall. This was the final cataclysm wherein both armies were destroyed, Mordred was slain and Arthur mortally wounded.

It was Arthur's failure to heed the warning of the dream of "The Dragon and Bear" that sealed his fate. But who was the great Bear of the dream? Had Merlin been there, he would have known that the Bear was in fact Arthur himself. As we delve into the relationship between the legendary King Arthur and the historic Dux Bellorum Artorius, we find that Arthur and Artorius are not only a phonetic match, they are literal translations as well: in both Celtic and Latin the words mean "bear." Furthermore, there is the rather remarkable fact that the star constellation

King Arthur defeats General Lucius and his Imperial Forces – but fails to conquer Rome because of Mordred's revolt.

known to the Greco-Romans (and to us) as the "Great Bear" was known to the Britons (and is still known to the Welsh) as "Arthur's Chariot." But accepting Arthur as the Bear in the dream, gives rise to an immediate problem because as King of the Britons Arthur was undeniably the Dragon (as was shown in the story of the "Red and the White Dragon"). So how could a battle take place, if the Bear and the Dragon were both Arthur? Herein lies the true message of the dream: it was a warning that Mordred would soon abuse the powers Arthur had given him by seizing the throne – and symbolically becoming the Dragon. The result was the disastrous struggle between the false Dragon (Mordred) and the Bear (Arthur). Arthur was certainly correct in his belief that the dream was of great importance, but his inability to understand its symbols was tragic in its consequences. It was a prophecy of the terrible civil war that would destroy both Arthur and Mordred, and bring fire and desolation to the Kingdom of the Britons.

By the early thirteenth century, the French composers of Arthurian Romances had added the spice of incest to Mordred's pedigree. Thereafter, he was not only King Arthur's nephew, but was also his son through an incestuous union with Arthur's half-sister, "Morgause." A couple of decades later, Mordred's family tree received its final graft: not only was he illegitimate and incestuously-conceived, but he was the unholy offspring of King Arthur and his sister, the inhuman enchantress Morgan Le Fay. Not surprisingly, it was this twisted manifestation of Mordred whose evil genius lay behind the murderous confrontation of the final battle.

The Battle of Camlann was emblematic of the end of the Arthurian age, and its stories fulfilled a requirement common to epic poetry and romance, whereby the lost golden age of heroes and heroines ends in cataclysm. In the *Iliad* Homer sang of the destruction of Troy, the slaughter of its people, and the obliteration of its civilization. In the Norse *Volsunga Saga* and the German epic of the *Nibelungenlied*, similar final conflicts end tragically with the extinction of the entire Volsung and Nibelung dynasties. We now know that Homer's

Sack of Troy – the cataclysmic end of the heroic age of Greece found an echo in Camlann, which ended the heroic age of Arthur's Britain.

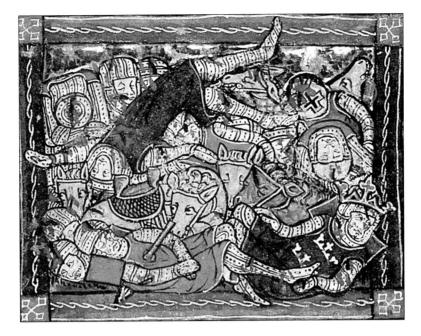

Iliad was based on the historical destruction of the Trojan nation in about 1100 BC and that both the *Volsunga Saga* and the *Nibelungenlied* were inspired by the historical annihilation of the Rhineland Burgundians by Attila's Huns in AD 437.

Similarly, Arthur's Battle at Camlann was a historical battle fought some time around AD 539. The tragic consequences of that battle grew in the imaginations of the bards because it symbolized the end of the dominion of the Britons. Elements of other historical battles were grafted onto the events of the Battle of Camlann to increase its fame. Certainly, the terrible and senseless Battle of Arderydd in AD 574 added a critical element to Arthur's story, for this was the battle at which the bard Myrddin Wyllt - Merlin the Wild - went mad at the sight of such slaughter of kinsmen, and fled into the wilderness. Then too, in the last year of the sixth century, the British bard Aneirin composed a lament for the Britons of the North Kingdom. From fragments alone, we know about this epic poem called *The Gododdin*. It tells of a military disaster in the last days of the sixth century, when the Britons of the North Kingdom made a brave last stand before the obliteration of their realm. The battle in this epic poem was fought sixty to eighty years after the Battle of Camlann, yet in spirit might be said to be the same battle: a last stand, fought again and again, as the People of the Red Dragon made their slow, stubborn retreat.

The repeated theme of the "Last Battle" was emblematic of the stoic heroism of the ancient Britons in the face of certain doom. Still, it must be acknowledged that the finest rendition of the "Last Battle" comes into the English language by way of Thomas Malory in the fifteenth century. Beyond the force of its language and directness of its speech, the *Morte*

The Battle of Camlann – became emblematic of the heroic stand of the Britons in the face of their certain doom.

d'Arthur has a pervading elegiac tone that is both tragic and beautiful. Malory was himself a knight who lived in a time when the flower of English armoured knighthood had been obliterated by French cannons, black death, famine, peasant revolt and civil war. The existence of gunpowder put in doubt any stability that armour and castle walls might have seemed to promise, and before its sulphurous breath the flower of chivalry withered and died. The last battle in Malory's *Morte d'Arthur* brought Arthur's Golden Age into direct contact with Malory's world during that form of national suicide that went by the name of the War of the Roses. It was a time of mindless slaughter wherein there were no victors, in which the moderation of good men went unheeded, and where cynical self-interest led directly to disaster. In King Arthur's last battle, we witness at once the eclipse of a mythic ideal kingdom, and a despairing allegory of the fate of fifteenth-century England.

Curiously, the hand of Merlin appears to have been at work in Malory's time. Several years after Malory's death, Britain's first publisher Caxton chose to edit and print the *Morte d'Arthur*. It was one of the first printed secular books in the English language. Even more remarkable, however, is the fact that it was published just three weeks before the final battle of the War of the Roses. This was the Battle of Boswell Fields, and the last battle ever to be fought by armoured knights in Britain. It was truly the end of an era.

The Battle of Boswell Fields – the historical last battle of the War of the Roses in 1485. By curious timing, Caxton published Malory's *Morte d'Arthur* in the same month.

CHAPTER FOURTEEN

THE ISLE OF AVALON

So Arthur spoke: "I go now unto the vale of Avilion to heal my grievous wounds."
Le Morte d'Arthur – *Malory*

Mortally wounded in the last battle of Camlann wherein all the best of the knighthood of Britain was extinguished, King Arthur commanded the last survivor, the loyal Sir Bedevere, to cast the sword Excalibur into the waters that lapped on the far edge of the battleground. When Excalibur was caught by the miraculous hand of a maiden and drawn into the depths, King Arthur knew that his duty was done and his destiny fulfilled. He felt the coldness of the earth creeping into his bones and the searing pain of his bloody wound, but the King knew his mortal suffering was nearing its end. In Malory's classic telling, Arthur is conveyed by a barge to his final resting place.

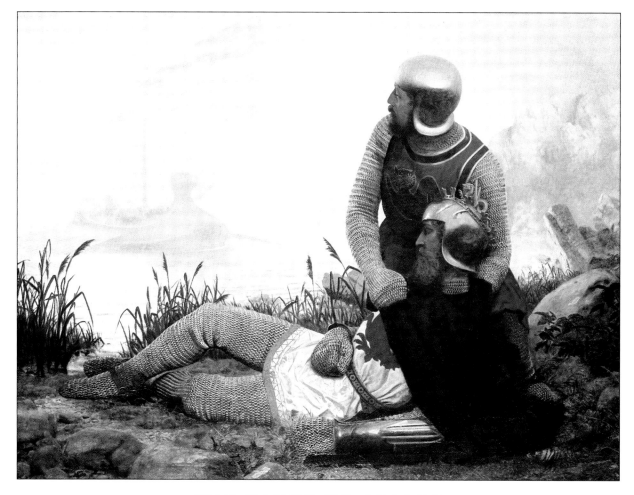

THE BARGE TO AVALON

In the twilight, a great swan-like black barge appeared upon the water bearing nine noble ladies all hooded in black. Among their number were three queens: Morgan Le Fay, the Queen of the Northgales and the Queen of the Waste Lands. And of the others, one was the King's guardian, the Lady of the Lake. With their healing hands these nine fair women lifted the wounded King up from the battle ground and took him to their barge to be carried far across the waters. Some say they ferried the King only to his grave. But in truth the nine sailed through the mists to the distant Isle of Avalon.

Arthur came to Avalon to heal his mortal wounds, and to find a place where his tortured soul might rest. The greatest of the nine queens, Morgan Le Fay, who is also Fate, took Arthur to her chamber and placed him upon a golden bed. For though Morgan and Arthur were rivals in the world of mortals, in Avalon Morgan became the instrument of his salvation. She uncovered and bathed Arthur's terrible gaping wounds. Then she used soothing ointments and whispered a healing spell as she bound them with linen.

Opposite **Loyal Knight – Sir Bedevere returns Excalibur to the lake.**
Above **The Wounded King – Arthur waits for the black barge of Morgan Le Fay that will take him to Avalon.**

Gently, she spoke to the King, saying it was within her powers to heal him, but his body and health would be restored only if he would remain in Avalon.

And so it is rumoured among the Britons since Arthur's passing that, with Morgan at his side, he remains in that earthly paradise where no harsh wind blows. In that faery kingdom, King Arthur holds court as once he did in Camelot. There all the heroes of the world gather and feast and have tournaments and all manner of sport and play. King Arthur waits in Avalon and watches the world. He watches the Britons and all the other folk of his realm. There he waits for the time of their greatest need – when he will come among them again.

Attending the King – the queens and their ladies attend the mortally wounded Arthur, before carrying him upon their barge and sailing to Avalon.

The Isle of Avalon has come to represent an enchanted realm just beyond our knowing, a refuge where all that was once mysterious and magical may still be found. Avalon is also the fountainhead of our inspiration and our dreams, the land of the nine queens, the nine Muses, the nine Graces, the nine Ladies of the Lake and all the handmaidens who serve those invisible forces that inspire all mortals. It is also a land where heroes of all ages gather, as the Knights of the Round Table once gathered in Camelot. Among the Vikings, it was the Valkyrie Battle Maidens who chose the heroes for their places in Valhalla. Indeed, Morgan Le Fay was frequently called the Queen of Avalon, but her isle, by whatever name it is known, has long since transcended strictly Arthurian legend and spread to all European cultures.

In the fourteenth-century Carolingian legend, *Chansons de Geste*, which tells about the court of Charlemagne, we find the greatest of the emperor's paladins, Ogier the Dane, entangled with Morgan Le Fay and stumbling upon the Isle of Avalon. The son of King Geoffrey of Denmark, Ogier is that country's national hero. His deeds were also celebrated in Ingemann's *Holger Danske* and many other epic cycles. In the nineteenth century, William Morris chose Ogier the Dane as the hero of his epic, *The Earthly Paradise*, as did the American poet Longfellow in his *Tales of a Wayside Inn*. In part, Ogier the Dane's adventure is based on one of the labours of Hercules who gathered the golden apples of the Hesperides, and eventually married Hebe, the goddess of eternal youth. In so doing, he became immortal.

MORGAN AND OGIER THE DANE

Ogier the Dane was numbered among the greatest heroes of the world. He knew the courts of Charlemagne, King Arthur, Attila the Hun, Dietrich von Berne and Saladin the Saracen, and he embarked on adventures that took him to far-off Jerusalem and even Babylon. In his hundredth year, on his return from Jerusalem Ogier went on one last quest to France but while at sea his ship was attacked by a vicious sea monster and dragged out into the wild ocean far beyond the Gates of Hercules. There a mighty storm drove the ship toward the rocky shore of a remote island. On that island was a towering rock made all of lodestone with a magnetic force so great that it ripped all the iron from the wooden hull of the ship. In no time at all, Ogier's ship was torn apart and the shattered masts, the smashed planks and the battered bodies of the drowned were strewn across the rocky shore. With the exception of the mighty Ogier the Dane, all perished that day in the wreck or upon the cruel rock.

With all his heroic companions lost, Ogier wandered about the island and discovered many strange and wonderful things. There was a castle of adamantine, invisible by day, but supernaturally radiant by night, and a magical and remarkable talking horse named Papillon, who was one of the most learned beings on the earth. Best of all,

Ogier found a beauteous garden. There he discovered a tree that bore golden apples and beneath it was the sleeping form of the most beautiful woman Ogier had ever seen. However, the tree was guarded by a great serpent whose coils wrapped menacingly around its trunk. Ogier drew his sword, Courtain, and slew the writhing monster with a single stroke. The fair woman revealed herself to be Morgan Le Fay, faery sister of King Arthur. Morgan had long sought Ogier the Dane, and she welcomed the old warrior to her realm. She kissed him, then placed a gold ring on his hand. Ogier felt instantly revitalized. By the power of Morgan's ring, he was granted eternal youth and immortality. Young and golden-haired once more, Ogier was overjoyed and so paid no attention when Morgan placed on his head a golden crown. This was the crown of oblivion, which caused Ogier to forget his homeland and all that lay beyond the island realm. Thereafter, Ogier wed Queen Morgan le Fay and they lived in a great castle, where they were joined by King Arthur, Tristan, Oberon and many other heroes. Through two hundred years of unchanging youth they enjoyed feasting and festivals and tournaments without end on the Isle of Avalon.

One day during a joust, the golden crown of oblivion was accidentally knocked off Ogier's head and the Dane suddenly remembered all his past and his duties in his homeland. Instantly, he mounted his wondrous horse, Papillon, and returned to France. Soon he entered the court of one of the Capetian kings of France who were the

Ogier the Dane – the Danish national hero who found immortality in Avalon as the husband of Morgan Le Fay.

heirs of Charlemagne. He was amazed by all that had changed in those two centuries that he had been away, but realized he had arrived just in time. Heroic as ever, Ogier stoutly organized the defence of Paris against the invading Normans. Blessed with eternal youth by the power of Morgan's magical ring, Ogier the Dane easily rode across France and Denmark, and set about righting the wrongs of the world. He served the Capetian king of France, as he had once done Charlemagne, and when the king died, Ogier prepared to marry the widow, and so become king of France himself. However, this was too much for Morgan Le Fay, and in the midst of the marriage ceremony the church foundations were rocked by a mighty thunderclap. Then there was a flash of light and Ogier the Dane found himself returned to Avalon, whence he, like King Arthur and Charlemagne, will remain, until once again his country needs him.

The name Avalon, Celtic for "Isle of Apples", reveals something of its origins. It is an earthly paradise and a second Eden; however, it was primarily inspired by Greek mythology, being modelled on the "Fortunate Isles" in the western sea where the wonderful Gardens of the Hesperides were to be found. The Hesperides were the nine daughters of the Titan named Atlas on whose shoulders the skies rested. His wife was Hesperis the goddess of the west. ("Hesperis" is Greek for "west.") Eventually the name "Hesperides" came to be

The "Fortunate Isles" of Greek Myth – the inspiration for Avalon. Also known as the Hesperides, the name for the nymphs who attended the Isle's tree of golden apples.

associated with the daughters and with the Western Isles. There were two chief wonders in the Gardens of the Hesperides. They had been wedding gifts to Zeus and Hera and were a magnificent tree that grew golden apples, and a spring of nectar – the wine of the gods – which made any who drank there young and immortal. These treasures embodied the universal wish that a newly married couple have health and wealth all the days of their lives. So precious were the fountain and the tree that Zeus decided to keep them far beyond the reach of mortals, on an island to the distant west of the Pillars of Hercules in the middle of the western ocean. There they were lovingly tended by the nine maidens, the Hesperides. Around the base of the tree was coiled the great serpent called Ladon who was guardian of the golden apples and the fountain.

In Greek mythology, the tale of the Hesperides or Western Isles was also bound up with that of Elysium, the Isle of the Blessed, where heroes chosen by the gods were rewarded after death. Instead of going to the subterranean world of shadows, the chosen ones walked upon the golden plain of the Elysian Fields. The Isles were under the sovereignty of the figure we now know as "Father Time" – Cronus, the god of time – and on their shores time stood still, the inhabitants were prosperous and immortal and the Golden Age that had vanished from the rest of the world remained intact. When Cronus ruled the Western Isles, he was not that grim and ancient "Father Time" but a youthful golden-haired king enthroned on the Isle of the Blessed.

Below and Opposite **Sleep of King Arthur – the guardian ladies and healing sisters attend the needs of the king in the hidden realm of Avalon.**

In such a heroes' paradise it was not surprising to find a sacred tree with golden apples on its boughs, and a wellspring of nectar at its root, for after life we are granted that which all desire during life: the gifts of infinite wealth and eternal youth.

During the Renaissance period the belief in the existence of these Isles was so great that many early explorers of the Americas went in search of them. In fact, the Spanish found the native cultures of Central and South America so rich in gold that they were inclined to believe that a tree with golden fruit might yet exist further inland. Certainly the expedition led by the Spanish explorer Ponce de Leon in what is now Florida was motivated by a quest for eternal life through the discovery of the fabled Fountain of Youth.

Geoffrey of Monmouth's mid-twelfth-century *Vita Merlini* offers one of the earliest descriptions of the Isle of Avalon, or Insula Pomorum ("Isle of Apples"). This was an isle of eternal summer warmth filled with self-propagating crops, and vines that sowed themselves. There, all dwelled in peace, without illness, and lived for longer than a hundred years. Here the wounded Arthur was taken after the battle of Camlanus. Geoffrey even gives us Avalon's precise geographic location: sailing westward on prevailing winds from the Pillars of Hercules and

through the Straits of Gibraltar, the Isle of Avalon could only be one of the Canary Islands, probably the largest, the Isle of Grand Canary.

Still, this was only one magician's opinion. There seems to be no shortage of suggested locations for Avalon and the list of candidates is long: Anglesey, Tory Island, Isle of Man (described in an ancient Irish legend as "Ablach," which is Gaelic for "rich in apples"), Bardsey Island (the Welsh local favourite, home of Arthur, Merlin and a magical cauldron that contained the long-lost "Twelve Treasures of the Ancient Britons"), Puffin Island, Iona Island (the Scottish Avalon called the "Isle of Dreams"), Gresholm, Aberystwyth, Gower, the Scilly Isles (believed to be ruled by Queen Morgan), and the tower of Avallon in Burgundy.

One of the most popular choices for Avalon is Glastonbury Tor, once an island surrounded by marsh water before the land was drained. It was claimed that there were once many apple trees there, hence, its "supporters" called it "Inis Avalon." However, there is no good evidence for Glastonbury ever having been called Avalon, except in two forged documents discovered at a much later date. Glastonbury was certainly called "Inis Witrin" or "Ynis Gutrin," both meaning "Isle of Glass" (which the Saxons called "Glastonbury") but whatever else Glastonbury might have been, it was not Avalon. The "discovery" of the grave and bones of King Arthur and Queen Guinevere at Glastonbury Abbey, not far from the Tor in AD 1190 was a medieval hoax perpetrated by the monks of the Abbey (with the help of Henry II) to attract pilgrims and their money to pay for its rebuilding and restoration after a disastrous fire. The numerous "legal" documents,

Arthur's "Burial Chamber" – one of a multitude of legendary burial sites of King Arthur. This massive cairn of ancient stone is known as Cefn Bryn near Reynoldson, Gower in Wales.

"historical" records and relics purporting to connect Glastonbury with Avalon or even with King Arthur, have all ultimately been proven to be forgeries mostly committed over a period of three centuries by the Glastonbury Abbey

monks. In other words, there is not one single piece of evidence to support the Glastonbury-Avalon connection.

Countless places are identified with Arthur's grave site, but in many Arthurian legends, the king is said to be alive still. Since before the year 1000 the return of Arthur has remained a constant source of debate. According to one Welsh folk tradition, he and his knights did not die but sleep in a cave beneath Snowdon, where they await a call from their country in its time of need; while at Cadbury Castle in Somerset, Arthur and his men are said to lie sleeping fully armed under the hill. Sometimes at night the beat of horses' hooves can be heard as they ride down to a spring. And in the north of England a legend says that Arthur and Guinevere sleep deep beneath Sewingshields Castle in Northumberland.

In the *Morte d'Arthur*, Thomas Malory allows King Arthur both to live on forever in Avalon, and to perish and be buried in the world of mortals. Arthur goes by barge to Avalon so his mortal wound may be healed. But that same night, Bedevere arrives at a chapel in Glastonbury where a hermit mourns by a fresh grave and tells him that, "at midnight, there came a number of ladies and brought here a corpse and paid me to bury him."

Glastonbury Tor – medieval forgeries and hoaxes perpetrated by the monks of Glastonbury Abbey have made this the most famous location for the legendary isle of Avalon.

Bedevere assumes it is Arthur, but Malory says others believe Arthur did not die. He himself says he does not know; he simply states that Arthur's

153

King Arthur Sleeps – beneath
mountain, castle or hill. The king
awaits the hour of our need,
when he will rise up and save
the nation.

life was changed that day, and that on his tomb was the inscription: "Here lies Arthur, King that was, King that is, King that will be again."

Wherever Avalon may be, in the popular mind it remains an island kingdom where Arthur still holds court today – with all the world's heroes gathered round him – just as once in Camelot. While we are confused and battered by the chaos of an ever-changing mortal world, King Arthur remains forever centred in the perfectly balanced peace of Avalon. No longer in conflict with earthly knights or unearthly spirits, the immortal Arthur can be the judge and arbiter of the ideals of our lives. Like a polestar in the sky, we may set the course of our lives by King Arthur's unwavering ideals. For he now lives in the rarefied atmosphere of the immortals – beyond all earthly desires and cares of the flesh.

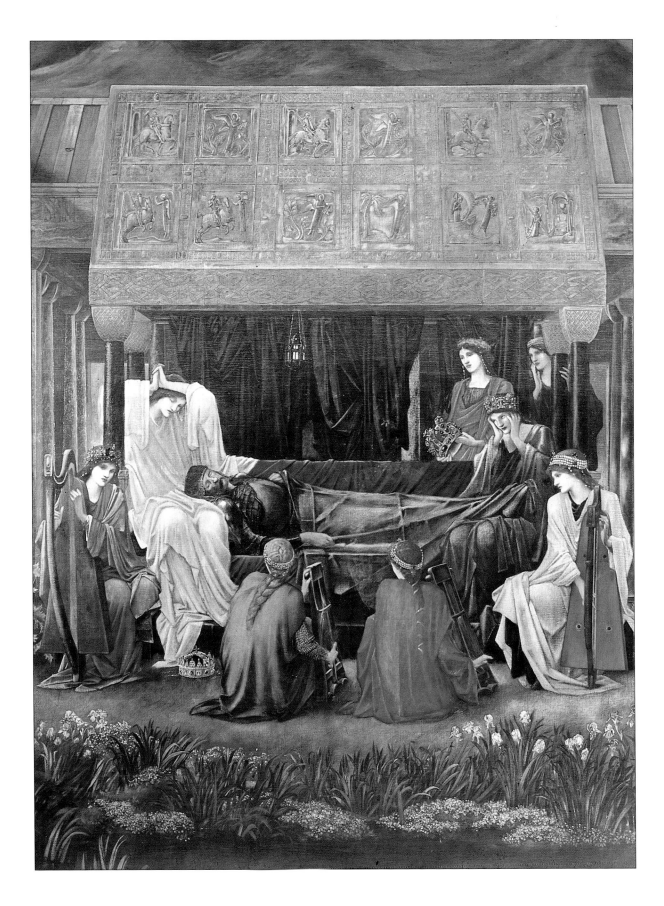

CHAPTER FIFTEEN

ONCE AND FUTURE KING

HIC IACET ARTHURUS, REX QUON DAM REX QUE FUTURUS.
Here lies Arthur – King that was, King that is, King that will be again.
Inscription on Arthur's tomb, from Le Morte d'Arthur *– Malory*

From the chaotic whirl of history, myth and legend that surrounds King Arthur there has emerged a body of literature that deals with nearly every aspect of human life. It has high tragedy and low comedy, high spiritual ideals and base material practicalities. In Arthur's world we see the spectacle and the horror of war in every form, from the most honourable to the most despicable and pointless. In stories of love, friendship and politics we see human suffering and human ecstasy in all their myriad manifestations: purity, nobility, constancy, passion, adultery, frivolity, incest, bestiality, rape, treachery, deceit, graft, corruption and murder. We meet creatures both monstrous and beautiful; we hear of wonderful visions and dire prophecies.

King Arthur is truly a hero for all ages. Most of the world's great heroic figures are trapped in a single place and time, but King Arthur's legend has crossed oceans and centuries to be endlessly reshaped by diverse hands. Among the ancient Britons, Arthur was a historic military commander who was the salvation of their nation and the greatest warrior of their race. Thus did Arthur become emblematic of the indomitable spirit of the Britons, an immortal leader who did not die, but retired to Avalon whence he might be summoned in his country's hour of need. Later, Arthur evolved into a British king whose court became a gathering place for the heroes of all the Celtic peoples. This Arthur was accepted by the Celts, the Normans and the Anglo-Saxons as a national hero, the ancient king of Britain and the archetypal monarch from whom all British kings claimed descent.

As King Arthur's Round Table became an ideal story-teller's vehicle by which heroes and tales from far-off lands might be given a unified theme and setting, so to Camelot came stories from every culture and civilization. King Arthur's figure was draped in the mantles of a multitude of heroes, from Alexander the Great to Charlemagne; from the Greek heroes Hercules and Theseus to the Norse Sigurd, the German Siegfried, the Irish

Hero For All Ages – King Arthur has been resurrected again and again over nearly fifteeen centuries as a tribal and national hero.

Cuchulain and the Anglo-Saxon Beowulf; from Achilles and Aeneas of the Trojan War to the heroes of ancient Israel and Babylon. Beyond these heroes, however, there was one other figure whose image we see clearly reflected in Arthur's and whose aura gave the King a special status: King Arthur eventually took on the messianic aspect of Jesus Christ. In the Middle Ages, King Arthur's Round Table was seen as a latter-day version of the table of the Last Supper. The clear implication was that Arthur was an earthly messiah betrayed by a Judas (Mordred) from among his disciples. Just as Christ was resurrected, so King Arthur was one day to return and be

the salvation of his people. As a militant Christ of the earthly kingdom, he would return to the mortal world and rebuild Camelot, an earthly manifestation of the New Jerusalem.

Not only did King Arthur approximate Christ in this messianic model, but he was also a Christ-like figure in that his "teachings" have far outlived his time on earth. Arthurian legend has come to be one of the prime vehicles for the propagation of the ideals of western civilization. King Arthur was seen as the greatest monarch of an age ruled by the ideals of chivalry and romantic love, and although these conventions were not invented by the authors of the Arthurian tradition, they were most vividly and famously conveyed therein. Chivalry in particular was an ideal that was only occasionally manifest in the often horrifically unchivalric medieval world, but in Arthur's realm its principles shone like a torch through the ages. However much chivalry might have been a cloak for a whole world of violence and self-interest, the Arthurian ideal was always a source of energy for selfless deeds and inspired art and literature.

From the school boy's sense of fair play to the rules of gentlemanly duels to the formalization of combat in boxing to protocols of peace, war and diplomacy; the largely fictional Arthurian model has shaped the history of the western world. For good or ill, it has led men to aspire to higher ideals of "knightly behaviour." And even though chivalry historically encouraged loyalty to an absolute monarch, over the years it has been democratized by the modern idea of nationhood. Indeed, patriotism – a heroic code of behaviour toward one's nation: the spirit of sacrifice, desire for justice, protection of the oppressed – is a direct descendant of chivalry.

This is the nature and purpose of a national hero and a national monarch. The whole point of a hereditary monarchy is to foster the illusion of continuity despite the reality of changing rulers. This basic tenet of monarchy is

Vision of Christ and the Grail – Arthur took on messianic aspects of Christ, and the Round Table became a latter-day table of the Last Supper.

conveyed in the seemingly paradoxical phrase, "the king is dead; long live the king." Thus as the "Once and Future King" King Arthur embodies this promise of a royal family's immortality and the implied promise of continuity and security. Britain's royal families have historically been perceived (or certainly they have tried to be perceived) as possessing a single unbroken immortal spirit. That spirit is King Arthur.

Historically, the elevation in status of Artorius the Dux Bellorum to the "Once and Future" King Arthur of the Britons was the result of the very real need of the British medieval kings to legitimize their royal claims. Since William the Conqueror in 1066, all royal dynasties that have seized power through force of arms have been compelled to provide evidence of their "divine selection." (Divine selection, along with the equally peculiar belief in the hereditary right to rule, was imposed by the ruling warrior class in medieval Europe to lend a veneer of stability to the seemingly – and violently – random social order of the day.) Without proof of divine selection, a monarch could not convince his subjects that he possessed the divine right to rule. And in most cases the de facto "evidence" for a British monarch's right to rule was the existence of a hereditary or mystical connection between that monarch and King Arthur. However, as no member of any British royal family has had even the remotest possibility of a blood tie with the historical Arthur, this illusion has variously been achieved by a combination of forged documents and genealogies, selective interpolation of already-existing chronicles and ancient mystical prophecies, and "discoveries" of ancient tombs.

An even simpler way to find a "historical" basis for a monarch's descent from King Arthur was to reward the court scholar who composed a new "history" – in the form of a popular romance or vernacular poem – that dramatized the desired claims. Indeed, the symbolic language of romance and poetry was an excellent medium for conveying the theme of an immortal king who was capable of mystical reincarnation. In essence, all that was required to establish descent from King Arthur was a poet's claim that his patron, the new monarch, was the original Arthur come again. This was certainly the case with William the Conqueror's descendant Henry I and even more so with Henry II, the founder of the Plantagenet line who, along with his wife Queen Eleanor of Aquitaine, so influenced Arthurian Romance. The romantic image of King Arthur was so resonant that even a diabolically bad king like Richard the Lion-Hearted was seen (and is still seen) as a good king because, like Arthur, he was a good soldier. Other Plantagenets, such as Edward I and

Richard I jousting with Saladin – the sword he claimed was Excalibur.

Edward III were perhaps more worthy of comparison with King Arthur, although it is difficult to see how beneficial their exploits in France ultimately proved to be. Each Plantagenet king worked very hard at being King Arthur Incarnate, and their colleagues worked overtime forging documents, relics and genealogies to prove their pedigree as heirs of Arthur.

When Henry Tudor emerged from the chaos of the War of the Roses and seized the English throne by right of conquest as Henry VII, his family's lineal claim to royal blood was dubious. He strengthened his case by marriage to Elizabeth Plantagenet, but knowing the value of legendary ancestry he also appointed a royal commission to consult British and Welsh books of pedigrees and they were able, not surprisingly, to present the king with "his perfect genealogy from the ancient kings of Britain." Henry VII's first son was christened Arthur, but the prince died young. His brother Henry VIII, however, picked up the Arthurian mantle with gusto, repairing the Round Table, festooning it with a large Tudor rose, and mounting it in the hall of Winchester Castle, which at the time was commonly believed to be the historical Camelot. In his youth Henry VIII was an impressive athlete and his banqueting house in Calais, known as the Field of the Cloth of Gold, was the scene of spectacular Arthurian tournaments. One ambassador to his court flattered Henry by observing his "nobleness and fame, which is greater than any prince since King Arthur."

It took a little imagination to portray a sovereign queen, Elizabeth I, as Arthur Incarnate, although had Elizabeth been a man, she would have made an excellent candidate for the position: she had sufficient Welsh blood to enable several genealogists to produce elaborately forged family trees tracing her directly back to King Arthur. It was in Elizabeth's court that Edmund Spenser composed the epic poem *The Faerie Queene* which was, quite naturally, modelled on the queen. In

Field of the Cloth of Gold – Henry VIII's spectacular Arthurian-style tournament in Calais was a royal pageant that increased his prestige.

the poem, Prince Arthur comes to the Queen's court as a knight in the days before he became king. Making sure no mistake is made, Spenser addresses Queen Elizabeth directly in the poem, just to confirm her pedigree:

> "Thy name, oh sovereign Queen, thy realm and race
> From this renowned Prince [Arthur] derived are."

In 1603, when the first of the Stuart kings, James I, ascended the English throne, he was greeted as the new King Arthur because he once again brought together Scotland, England and Wales as one nation of Great Britain. But the Stuarts were as destructive to the Arthurian legend as they were to the institution of the British monarchy. A good part of the Stuarts' extremely high-handed position on the divine right of kings was based on the historical truth of King Arthur and all the British kings' descent from him through William the Conqueror. Thus they forced the parliamentary faction to take a serious look at the genealogies of the monarchy and the historical records for King Arthur. Of course, historical evidence was either non-existent or legally fraudulent, and both the Stuarts and Arthur's prestige suffered under the scrutiny. The monarchy was ridiculed and the idea of tracing descent from Arthur was seen as a joke.

As a legal force in the selection of the monarch, King Arthur's powers began to wane in earnest with the execution of Charles I. With the obliteration of the monarchy, Parliament began to look to Anglo-Saxon and Common Law as the basis for the king's right to rule.

Court of the Faerie Queene – Elizabeth I was the model for Edmund Spenser's epic poem about the ideal Arthurian queen.

Unfortunately, Arthur had been so closely linked with the divine right of kings, that his legend fell from favour. (In truth, the historical Arthur had much more in common with the monarchy's arch-enemy, the "anti-Arthur" Oliver Cromwell, than with Charles I: Arthur the Dux Bellorum was no king but, like Cromwell, a cavalry officer *par excellence* who was able to rally the support of his peers.) When the monarchy in the person of Charles II was restored in 1660, a book of prophecies appeared that contained the genealogy of "His Highness's Lineal Descent from the Ancient Prince of Britain, clearly manifesting that He is the Conqueror they so long prophesied." Such prophecies notwithstanding, King Arthur's name never regained its legal stature. Lacking both historical veracity and relevance to the royal succession, his appeal as a subject of epic tales dwindled, and claims of royal descent from King Arthur were never taken entirely seriously again.

Although there were some minor works on Arthur, to all intents and purposes the king slumbered undisturbed in Avalon until the middle of the nineteenth century, when he returned with the force of a thunderbolt: Alfred Lord Tennyson's massive epic poem *Idylls of the King* − after Malory's *Morte d'Arthur*, the most important work in Arthurian literature. Tennyson's combination of lyric medievalism with Victorian morality and bourgeois values proved immensely popular. His Arthur is the Victorian spirit of rational self-control "working out his will to cleanse the world." It is very likely that Tennyson's *Idylls* saved the British monarchy from the republican movement, as it has been credited with giving the English a sympathetic portrait of the until then highly unpopular and autocratic German husband of Queen Victoria, Prince Albert. Had it not been for Tennyson's *Idylls* injecting some sense of romance into the sadly flagging image of the royal family, the monarchy might well have ended with Queen Victoria.

Anti-Arthur − Oliver Cromwell, like the historical Artorius, was the supreme soldier, but his rise signalled Arthur's and the monarchy's decline.

As far as Arthurian literature was concerned, Tennyson opened the floodgates, and the flow has not stopped from his day to ours. Tennyson's revival of King Arthur coincided with the expansion of the British Empire across the globe, and from America to Africa, India to Australia, in novels, poems, stories, plays, fairy tales, drawings and paintings, Tennyson – along with Malory – inspired thousands of writers and artists worldwide to tell the tale of England's greatest hero. Master Victorian and Pre-Raphaelite painters took up Arthurian themes with passion and freshness of vision. A new era of creative Arthurian scholarship dawned, and poets as varied as Sir Walter Scott, William Wordsworth, Charles Swinburne, William Morris and Henry Wadsworth Longfellow wrote long Arthurian poems and tales. Less worshipfully, Mark Twain's irreverent send-up of Camelot, *A Connecticut Yankee in King Arthur's Court*, is considered one of America's best satiric novels.

As the twentieth century rolled around, the public enthusiasm for Arthurian literature increased still further. In the first decades of the century, Arthur appeared in everything from juvenilia to scholarly historical and sociological studies by Jessie Weston, Roger Sherman Loomis and E K. Chambers. In poetry, the Arthurian legend reached its pinnacle in T.S. Eliot's masterpiece *The Wasteland* which in its symbolism, structure and theme is based on the Arthurian Quest of the Holy Grail. In both World Wars the spirit of King Arthur was summoned often, for Britain was certainly in her time of need. Propaganda posters, popular literature and motion pictures brought back the "Once and Future King" again and again. None were more clearly seen as Arthurian knights than that elite brotherhood of air aces who fought in the Battle of Britain during World War II. It seemed to many Britons, from Winston Churchill down, that in this miraculous battle, the spirit of Arthur and his knights took to the air like a fleet of avenging angels to defend England in her darkest hour. The impossible was indeed achieved when those daring few duelled with the German forces in the air above England and drove back the dark tide of the German invaders, just as surely as the legendary Arthur had done in the fifth century. (Not that the Germans missed any opportunity to benefit from Arthur's largesse. Arthurian literature has permeated German culture from medieval times, and one of Richard Wagner's greatest operas, *Parsifal*, was based on the Arthurian Grail Quest. In the midst of the war, Hitler sent several of his high-ranking SS officers on a secret mission to recover the Holy Grail. Following clues from *Parsifal* and earlier

Victoria and Albert – rulers saved from republicanism largely through the renewed public interest in royalty generated by Tennyson's *Idylls of the King*.

medieval German Arthurian scholars and poets, the party went on an expedition to Montsegur in the Pyrenees where legend placed the Grail Castle. The mission failed.)

In the fifties, two of the most celebrated and ambitious Arthurian novels of the century were produced by Oxbridge dons. T.H. White wrote his fresh, colloquial and purposely anachronistic *The Once and Future King*, while J.R.R. Tolkien's huge three-volume novel, *The Lord of the Rings*, was an epic fantasy that rivalled Spenser's *The Faerie Queene* in its originality and grandeur.

These works were followed by thousands of novels and critical studies. King Arthur has become a hero who can be adapted to promote almost any cause: Marion Zimmer Bradley's novel *The Mists of Avalon* and Norma Lorre Goodrich's *Guinevere* present the Arthurian world from a feminist perspective. John Heath-Stubbs's epic poem *Artorius* presents a Romano-Celtic Arthur; Nikolai Tolstoy's *In Search of Merlin* explores the magician's shamanic roots; and Jean Markale in his *King of the Celts* takes a Marxist approach.

In film, the Arthurian Grail Quest serves as an effective form of psychotherapy in the contemporary setting of Terry Gilliam's *The Fisher King*. *Star Wars* transports Arthur and Merlin far into the future, and out into space, where they are transformed into Luke Skywalker and Obi-wan Konobi. One wonders what the real Arthur (or Geoffrey of Monmouth, or Malory or Tennyson) would have made of the light-hearted Disney animated feature version of T. H. White's *The Sword In the Stone*, the dry-iced and flood-lit Camelot of John Boorman's *Excalibur*, or the twentieth-century Grail Quest embarked on in *Indiana Jones and the Last Crusade*. But the challenges faced by Indiana Jones and his father pale in comparison with those endured by the bold knights of *Monty Python and the Holy Grail*. Despite these rather loose translations of Arthur's story, the traditional role of King Arthur as a provider of pedigrees for monarchs and aristocrats has not been entirely abandoned. In their *King Arthur: the True Story*, Graham Phillips and Martin Keatman provide several prominent Welsh, Scots and Warwick families with suggested Arthurian ancestors. And Geoffrey Ashe takes a giant leap backward in emulation of Geoffrey of Monmouth in his *Discovering Arthur* wherein he (with the help of *Debrett's Peerage*) attempts to trace the Windsor family back to King Arthur. (He adds, hopefully, that as the current Prince Harry's middle name is Arthur, the prince could, if he wished, eventually become King Arthur II.)

Arthurian Quest – the search has continued even into this century: Hitler sent officers to the Pyrenees in the hope of finding the Grail.

It's a contagious thing, this Arthurian heritage. President John F. Kennedy and his family apparently felt an affinity with King Arthur after seeing several performances of Lerner and Loewe's musical stage play *Camelot*. With considerable success, the family and their publicists worked to project the image of the Kennedy years at the White House as an idyllic Utopian period of American history. And there is no denying that the Arthurian heritage still has force, so much so, for example, that thirty years later President Bill Clinton, seeing in Kennedy the closest thing to an American "Once and Future King," modelled his 1993 Presidential Inauguration on President Kennedy's own Camelot-inspired celebrations.

If nothing else, our long quest for King Arthur forces us to understand one thing: like the kings and queens of England, we all invent our own heritage and create our own pedigrees. We can see from the evolution of Arthur's story that both history and myth are acts of imagination and choice, and that both have the same purpose – self-definition. As nations and as individuals, we are free to choose our own history and our own myths, and in so doing, we create the world we live in.

From the fifth century to the twentieth, King Arthur has been recreated thousands of times, for not only must the Once and Future King return with each age, but the towers of his kingdom of Camelot must be continually raised with that wizard power we call the human imagination. Utopian ideals are ever-changing in a mortal world. The eternal Camelot must be refashioned and the Once and Future King reshaped. King Arthur continues to be an ever-shifting entity: turbulent, whirling - a cyclone.

AN ARTHURIAN CHRONOLOGY AND SELECTED BIBLIOGRAPHY

BC

*c.*1200 Celtic peoples settle in British Isles (Britons or proto-Welsh-speaking Celts in Britain, Gaels or proto-Irish-speaking Celts in Ireland).

Trojan War: Legendary Trojan prince Aeneas flees Troy for Rome and becomes the progenitor of the founders of Rome (according to Virgil), and Britain (according to Geoffrey of Monmouth).

*c.*1000 Legendary King Brutus, great-grandson of Aeneas, becomes founder and first king of Britain.

*c.*750 Romulus and Remus, legendary founders of Rome.

Homer's oral epic poems the *Iliad* and the *Odyssey* composed, although not written down until c.600 BC.

*c.*400 Belinus and Brennius, legendary British kings, defeat the Imperial Roman army and sack Rome (according to Geoffrey of Monmouth).

*c.*330 Conquests of Alexander the Great from Greece to India.

*c.*100 King Lud, legendary king of Britain, builds walls of London or "Lud-town" (according to Geoffrey of Monmouth).

55 Julius Caesar leads first Roman invasion of Britain.

20 Virgil writes his epic poem the *Aeneid.*

AD

10 Livy writes his *History of Rome.*

43 Roman conquest of Britain by Emperor Claudius. By AD 47 Britain has become a province of the Roman Empire and remains so for nearly four centuries.

60 Briton Queen Boudicca's revolt.

*c.*100 Official orders of Roman Equestrian Knights instituted among young Roman aristocrats, who swear to serve the Emperor and the Empire.

*c.*120 Hadrian's Wall built, from Carlisle to Newcastle (Solway Firth to Tynemouth.) Roman-Briton alliance with the "Twelve Kings of the North" keeps the peace and the Picts, Scots and Saxons at bay for the next two centuries.

*c.*140 Antonine Wall built, from Glasgow to Edinburgh (Firth of Clyde to Firth of Forth)

*c.*160 Lucius Artorius Castus commands the Roman Sixth Legion Sarmatian cavalry posted first in Brittany, then in Britain at Hadrian's Wall.

*c.*208 Roman dominion in Britain under Severus (temporarily) extends as far north as Aberdeen.

212 Emperor Caracalla grants all Britons Roman citizenship.

*c.*290 King Coel, legendary ruler of the four tribes of the North Kingdom and the model for the "Old King Cole" of nursery rhymes.

*c.*320 Constantine the Great founds Constantinople.

378 Battle of Adrianople: Visigoth barbarian cavalry defeats Roman Legion.

*c.*380 Heavy assaults by Scots, Picts and Saxons on Roman and Briton fortifications. Roman Legion forces in Britain number sixty thousand.

*c.*390 Roman Empire divides into East (Constantinople) and West (Rome).

406 Visigoth invasion of Italy. Emperor Honorius orders Roman troops withdrawn from Britain.

410 Sack of Rome by Alaric the Visigoth. Last of legions withdraw from Britain, but Roman governor appointed to organize Britons.

418 Last Roman governor abandons Britain, and the Emperor declares Britain an independent state. Authority returns to ancient Celtic tribal chiefs, loosely organized under an overlord, or "Vortigern."

436 Annihilation of the powerful Rhineland Germans, the Burgundians by a Roman-hired contingent of Attila the Hun's forces.

448 Britons appeal to Roman Consul of Gaul in face of invading Picts, Scots and Saxons. No reply, as Gaul is herself under attack by the Huns.

451 Attila's Huns are defeated by a Roman-barbarian army.

455 Vandals sack Rome.

*c.*460 Saxon Revolt: Mercenary Anglo-Saxons join with Picts and Scots against Britons – the basis of the legendary Vortigern's alliance with Hengist and Horsa.

476 Final collapse of western Roman Empire. Barbarian cavalries crush the Imperial army in Italy. Gaul divided into Frankish kingdoms.

*c.*480 Ambrosius Aurelianus, historical Roman who becomes governor, restores old Roman order and brings peace and prosperity to Britain.

490-500 The historical Artorius Dux Bellorum leads Britons to twelve victories against Saxons, Picts and Scots, ending in the battle of Mons Badonicus (Badon Hill).

500 "Peace of Arthur" lasts for 20 to 40 years – the legendary Golden Age of Camelot.

516 *Lex Burgundionum*, the earliest written account of events of the Burgundian massacre of AD 436 and the basis of the *Nibelungenlied* and the *Volsunga Saga*.

*c.*539 Battle of Camlann. The place, participants and exact date for this battle are debated but there *was* a historical battle, probably near Hadrian's Wall. According to legend this was the final conflict betwen Arthur and Mordred.

*c.*546 Saint Gildas writes *De Excidio Britanniae* (*The Ruin of Britain*).

574 Merlin the Wild (Myrddin Wyllt), the historical Briton bard, goes mad at the Battle of Arfderydd (Arthuret) and flees into the forest.

c.580 Britons defeated by Saxons at Dyrham, Bath, Cirencester and Gloucester.

598 Angle kings defeat Britons at Battle of Catterick in York.

*c.*600 Aneirin composes the Briton epic poem *The Gododdin*.

613 Death of historical Visigoth Queen Brunhilda, the model for the murderous queens of the *Nibelungenlied* and the *Volsunga Saga*.

*c.*650 Sacking of Briton kingdoms of Powys, Dyfed, Gododdin, Gwent. Devon absorbed by Wessex.

*c.*720 *Beowulf,* the oral epic poem, is composed.

*c.*730 Venerable Bede, the Anglo Saxon scribe writes *Historia Ecclesiastica Gentis Anglorum* (*The History of the English Church and People).*

*c.*760 King Offa of Mercia builds the 150 mile-long Offa's Dyke to wall off the Briton tribes of Wales.

*c.*800 Charlemagne of the Franks is crowned Holy Roman Emperor.

*c.*810 Nennius writes *Historia Brittonum* (*The History of the Britons*). First list of Arthur's deeds and battles.

c.850 Viking raiders attack Anglo-Saxon and European settlements all over coastal Europe.

900 Charlemagne's Holy Roman Empire splits up into three parts, roughly equivalent to France, Italy and Germany

926 King Athelstan becomes first king of the Anglo-Saxons of Britain.

c.937 Briton kingdoms of Cornwall and the Strathclyde finally come under Anglo-Saxon control.

c.950 Norse *Volsunga Saga* is composed based on earlier Germanic oral epic compositions.

c.956 *Annales Cambriae (The Annals of Wales)* first written down (although this anonymous manuscript has been lost).

c.1000 *Chansons de Gestes* composed. These oral French poems relate the deeds of Charlemagne and his paladins (knights)

c.1017 King Canute rules England, Denmark, Norway and southern Sweden.

1065 Tournaments are held that formalize rules of combat and a code of knightly behaviour that the Normans call "chivalrie"(horsemanship).

1066 William the Conqueror is victorious at the Battle of Hastings. A comet appears in the sky during the Norman invasion.

1086 William compiles his *Domesday Book*, the first national census of Britain. After their ruthless pacification of the Saxons and a massive castle-building programme, the Norman occupation becomes permanent.

1095 First Crusade is launched by Pope Urban II.

1098 Cisterican Order is founded in France.

c.1100 Troubadours, court minstrels originally from Provencal in Southern France, more or less invent "romantic love." Their romantic poetry flourishes until 1350.

1100 Henry I becomes king of England.

1120 Compilation of earliest surviving manuscript containing the *Annnales Cambriae* and Nennius's *Brittonum Historia*.

1128 Templar Knights (Cistercian warrior-monks) receive papal recognition through the influence of Bernard of Clairvaux who drafts their rules of conduct.

1136 Geoffrey of Monmouth writes *Historia Regum Britanniae (The History of the Kings of Britain)*, containing the first full-length life story of King Arthur.

c.1140 The historical philosopher Peter Abelard is convicted of heresy and inspires the tale of Abelard and Heloise.

1147 Second Crusade instigated by Bernard of Clairvaux.

Eleanor of Aquitaine, Queen of France, embarks on crusade with her first husband, Louis, King of France.

1148 Geoffrey of Monmouth writes *Vita Merlini (The Life of Merlin)*.

c.1150 Arthurian Romance: cycles of poems and prose adventure tales set in King Arthur's court are composed in vernacular French.

Henry II becomes first Plantaganet king of England. His wife Eleanor of Aquitaine (once married to Louis of France) becomes Queen of England.

c.1155 Robert Wace writes *Le Roman de Brut*, a Norman-French poem based on Geoffrey of Monmouth's *History*, which includes the first mention of the Round Table Knights. Dedicated to Queen Eleanor of Aquitaine.

c.1160 Thomas de Britagne composes *Tristan*, a Plantagenet court version of the Tristan legend which combines Greek and Arthurian mythology.

Anonymous *Dream of Rhonbury*; Welsh poem in which a knight dreams of the "Emperor Arthur".

*c.*1170 *Draco Narmannicus* (*The Norman Standard*): Etienne de Rouen composes this Breton French account of a living King Arthur in Avalon writing a letter to Henry II in which he advises him to treat the Bretons better.

*c.*1172 Chretien de Troye writes *Lancelot* or *Le Chevalier a la Cherrette* (*The Knight of the Cart*) which introduces Lancelot the Breton French knight and for the first time names the kingdom of Camelot. "The Ordeal of the Sword Bridge" (in which Lancelot heroically rescues Guinevere) is commissioned by Marie de Champaigne.

*c.*1183 In the *Prophetia Anglicana*, Alain de Lille reports fights and stonings in Briton market towns when foreigners refute the local belief that King Arthur lives still in Avalon.

1185 Chretien de Troyes writes *Perceval* or *Le Conte du Graal*.

Andreas Capellanus writes *The Art of Courtly Love*, which conveys the idea of romantic sexual love as an ennobling force.

1189 Richard the Lion-Heart becomes king of England. He immediately empties the country's coffers to finance the Third Crusade during which he honours King Tancred of Sicily by presenting the Norman king with Richard's family heirloom, King Arthur's sword Excalibur.

Marie de France writes the *Lay of Sir Launfal*.

1190 Layamon writes *Brut*, the first English saga about Arthur; based on Geoffrey of Monmouth by way of Robert Wace.

1191 Geraldus Cambrensis visits the graves of Arthur and Guinevere at Glastonbury which were "discovered" the previous year.

*c.*1200 Robert de Boron writes *Le Roman du Saint Graal* which portrays the Holy Grail as a dish from the Last Supper which Joseph of Arimathea brought to Britain.

*c.*1200 The *Nibelungenlied*, the German national epic based on the fifth-century annihilation of the Rhineland Burgundians, is composed anonymously.

1205 Wolfram von Eschenbach writes *Parzival*, a German epic partly based on Chretien. Wolfram identifies Templar crusaders as modern Grail knights.

1210 Gottfried von Strassburg writes *Tristan and Isolde*, a German reworking of the Tristan legend.

1215-35 Cistercian scribes compile the *Prose Lancelot* or *The Vulgate Cycle*, a massive French prose volume.

King John signs the Magna Carta

1247 *De Antiquitate Glastoniensis*: This faked document is forged by the monks of Glastonbury to prove a connection between Glastonbury, Arthur and the Holy Grail.

*c.*1250 *Black Book of Carmarthen* written. This is the oldest surviving collection of Welsh Arthurian poetry, including poems attributed to the sixth-century Welsh bard Merlin the Wild (Myrddin Wyllt).

*c.*1265 *Book of Aneirin* written. It contains the oldest surviving copy of the sixth-century epic poem *The Gododdin*, attributed to the Welsh bard Aneirin.

*c.*1275 *Book of Taliesin* written. Stories attributed to the sixth-century Welsh bard Taliesin portray Arthur as questing mythic hero.

*c.*1300 Dante writes his *Divine Comedy*.

1337 Start of the Hundred Years War. Use of longbows and artillery make armoured knights increasingly obsolete.

1347 The Black Death: bubonic plague kills a third of Europe's population.

1349 Edward III founds the Order of the Knights of the Garter.

*c.*1360 *The Morte Arthure*, an alliterative dialect stanzaic poem written by an anonymous Scotsman.

*c.*1390 *Sir Gawain and the Green Knight*, an alliterative poem, written by an anonymous poet (the "Gawain Poet") in the northwest Midlands.

*c.*1430 Suits of armour replace chain mail, but gunpowder changes everything. Armoured knights and chivalry become increasingly obsolete.

*c.*1440 *The Romance of Sir Perceval of Galles* written by Robert Thornton. In this English-language romance, King Arthur is modelled on Edward III.

1450 The beginnings of the Italian Renaissance and the Protestant Reformation.

1453 The Hundred Years War ends with English humiliation in the face of French artillery at Bordeaux.

1454 The Guttenberg Bible inaugurates era of mass book production.

1455 The War of the Roses begins.

1470 While in prison for murder, rape, robbery and pillaging, Sir Thomas Malory writes *Le Morte d'Arthur.*

1485 Caxton publishes *Le Morte d'Arthur* just three weeks before the Battle of Boswell Fields which ends the War of Roses. Henry VII becomes the first king of the Tudor dynasty.

1500 Henry VIII becomes king of England.

1554 Holinshed publishes an expanded version of *The Prophecies of Merlin.*

1555 Michel de Nostradamus's book *Centuries* is published. His prophecies will eventually surpass Merlin's in popularity.

1582 *The Assertion of the Most Noble Arthur* by John Leland is published, fiercely defending the historicity of Arthur.

1596 Edmund Spenser composes *The Faerie Queene* in which Arthur is a knight in the dazzling court of the Faerie Queene, modelled on Elizabeth I.

1613 Ben Jonson writes *The Lord's Masque* for King James's son and heir Prince Henry whose character is "Arturus, once thy King and now thy star."

1641 Thomas Heywood writes *The Life of Merlin,* which features Heywood's interpretation of the Merlin's prophecies.

1642 English Civil War begins with conflict between Royalist and Parliamentarian forces. Cromwell's New Model Army proves superior.

1644 William Lilly edits and publishes *Merlinus Anglicanus Junior,* a book of prophecies attributed to Merlin that tells of then current events.

1660 Restoration of the British monarchy with Charles II's accession to the throne.

1691 Dryden and Purcell compose the opera *King Arthur,* a fantasy about Arthur and the blind Princess Emmeline unrelated to any known legend.

1700 Sir Richard Blackmore writes *King Arthur,* an attempt at heroic epic poetry by William III's physician. Arthur is patterned on William of Orange, an ardent Protestant, and Satan is aligned with supporters of Catholic Stuarts.

1777 Thomas Warton's long poem *The Grave of King Arthur* is drawn from accounts of the "discovery" at Glastonbury.

1804 Sir Walter Scott writes *Sir Tristam,* a medieval variation on the Tristan legend.

1815 *Beowulf* is published for the first time.

Malory's *Morte d'Arthur* is reprinted for the first time in nearly two hundred years. This edition, with a preface by Robert Southey, is a major influence on Tennyson.

1825 Joseph Ritson's *Life of King Arthur* is the first solid critical and historical examination of Arthur's life.

1832 *The Lady of Shalott* is Alfred Lord Tennyson's first Arthurian poem.

1842 Tennyson writes the first volume of his massively popular epic *Idylls of the King* in which King Arthur is refashioned as a gentleman with Victorian moral values. Tennyson continues writing this poetry cycle until 1888.

1853 Tennyson's *The Charge of the Light Brigade* responds to events in the Crimean War. Arthurian chivalry and Victorian cavalry virtues become interchangeable.

1858 William Morris's long poem *The Defence of Guinevere* is a reply to Tennyson's moralizing condemnation of Arthur's queen.

1868 W.F. Skene edits the *Four Ancient books of Wales* in Edinburgh. He was the first scholar to locate King Arthur's North Kingdom of the Gododdin between Hadrian and Antonine Walls.

1870 William Morris's first translation of the Icelandic *Volsunga Saga*, referred to as the "Iliad of the North".

1876 First performance of Richard Wagner's opera *The Ring of the Nibelung*. (His other operas include *Tristan and Isolde* and *Parsifal*.)

1882 Charles Algernon Swinburne's poem *Tristram of Lyonesse* passionately retells the much-told romance.

1889 Mark Twain's *A Connecticut Yankee in King Arthur's Court* satirizes both Arthur's time and Twain's.

1892 William Morris's Kelmscott Press publishes an illustrated edition of Malory's *Morte d'Arthur* that is among the most beautiful books ever printed.

1920 Jessie L. Weston's *From Ritual to Romance* is the first analysis of the Grail legend that uses cultural anthropology and Jungian psychology.

1922 T.S. Eliot's writes *The Wasteland*, influenced by Weston's research.

1926 Roger Sherman Loomis's *Celtic Myth and Arthurian Romance* emphasizes the Celtic contribution to Arthurian literature.

1927 E.K. Chambers's *Arthur of Britain* is the most thorough early scholarly investigation of the historic Arthur and his literary and mythic origins.

1940 Battle of Britain fought between German and British air forces.

1955 In his epic *Lord of the Rings*, J.R.R. Tolkien creates a mythology that shares major themes and archetypal characters with the Arthurian legend.

1958 T.H. White's *Once and Future King* is a colloquial and consciously anachronistic take on Camelot.

1960 Broadway opening of Lerner and Loewe's *Camelot*, based on T.H. White. The musical inspires the Kennedys to fashion JFK's presidency (1961-63) after Arthur's Utopian reign.

Films 1967-to present day The film version of *Camelot* (1967) is released and King Arthur once again rides into the public imagination. During the next three decades movies with an Arthurian theme proliferate, including *Monty Python and the Holy Grail* (1974), *Star Wars* (1977), *Excalibur* (1981), *Indiana Jones and the Last Crusade* (1989), *The Fisher King* (1991) and *First Knight (1995)*.

Fiction 1970-present day Publication of Mary Stewart's popular historical romance *The Crystal Cave* (1970), the first volume in an Arthurian series. Other popular fictional works on Arthur include Marion Zimmer Bradley's *The Mists of Avalon* (1981), a feminist fantasy based on the Arthurian legend, and Deepak Chopra's *The Return of Merlin (*1973). John Heath-Stubbs's *Artorius* is an epic poem based on the historical Romano-Celtic Arthur.

Critical Studies 1977-present day Jean Markale's (Marxist) *King of the Celts* is published (1977). Arthurian scholarship continues with, among others, Nikolai Tolstoy's *The Quest for Merlin* (1985), Norma Lorre Goodrich's *Arthur (1986), Merlin (1988)* and *Guinevere (1991)*, Geoffrey Ashe's *Discovery of King Arthur* (1985) and Graham Phillips and Martin Keatman's *King Arthur: The True Story (1994)*.

INDEX

Picture Credits

l - left, r - right, t - top, b - bottom

Front jacket – Bridgeman Art Library/Sheffield City Art Galleries, Thomas Jones Barker: *The Faithful Knight*
Jacket flap Arthur Rackham: *Arthur and Mordred* from *The Romance of King Arthur*
1 Arthur Rackham: dragon motif from *The Romance of King Arthur*
2-3 Arthur Rackham: *Knight* from *The Romance of King Arthur*
6-7 background Mary Evans Picture Library. Gustave Doré: *The Knights Carouse* from Tennyson's *Idylls of the King*
8 © Alan Lee
10 AKG London. Friedrich Emil Klein: *Attila the Hun, 1890*
12 Jean-Loup Charmet. Raymond de la Marre: *Attila the Hun* from *La Petite Histoire de la France, 1942*
13 Ben Russell Warner
14 © Alan Lee
15 Bridgeman Art Library/British Library, London. *King Arthur and the Thirty Kingdoms*, Peter Langtoft *Chronicle of England*, MS Royal 20 A II, f. 4r
16 Mary Evans Picture Library. Gustave Doré: *The Knight's Progress* from Tennyson's *Idylls of the King*
18 Janet and Colin Bord/Fortean Picture Library. Hadrian's Wall on Walltown Crags, Northumberland
19 © Alan Lee
21 Bridgeman Art Library/Forbes Magazine Collection. Henry Clarence Whaite: *Arthur in the Gruesome Glen*
23 © Alan Lee
24 Bodleian Library, Oxford. *Birth of Merlin*
25 Lambeth Palace Library, London. *Merlin interpreting a scene showing the Red Dragon and the White Dragon to Vortigern*, MS 6 f.43v
27 Fine Art Photographic Library/Julian Simon Fine Art, London. Benjamin Haydon: *Slaying the Dragon*
28 Mick Sharp. Llyn Dinas & River Glaslyn, Nantgwynant, Gwynedd
29b Ancient Art & Architecture. *Kings Alfred, Arthur and Canute*. Stained glass at Winchester Cathedral
31 Walter Crane: *Arthur Draws the Sword from the Stone*
32 Mary Evans Picture Library. Arthur Rackham: *Little People of the mountains* from Wagner's *Siegfried*
33 AKG London/Palazzo Vecchio, Florence. Jan Stradanus Alchemy, 1570
35 © Alan Lee
36 ET Archive/Oldsaksammlung, Oslo. Carved wooden panel from Hylestad stave church doorway, 12th cent.
37 Early 3rd-cent. grafitto of Sarmatian cavalry from Hadrian's Wall
38 Bridgeman Art Library/Bradford Art Galleries & Museums. *King Arthur*, stained glass window by William Morris & Co
40 ET Archive/British Library, London. Matthew Paris: Miniature of Norman kings from *Historia Anglorum*
41 Bodleian Library, Oxford. Illuminated page from Geoffrey of Monmouth's *Gesta Regium Britanniae* Ms Lat Misc.e.42 f. 27
42 ET Archive/Victoria & Albert Museum. Tapestry made at Tournai, 1475-90, showing the *Trojan War*
43l British Library, London. *Vortigern on the Castle in Flames* from Peter Langtoft *Chronicle of England* MS Royal 20 AII f.3

43r Bodleian Library, Oxford. Illuminated page from Geoffrey of Monmouth's *Gesta regum Britanniae* MS Lat Misc.e.42 f. 39
44 AKG London/Bibliotheque Nationale, Paris. *Merlin dictating to Blaise, his Scribe* from Robert de Boron's *Histoire de Merlin* MS Francaise 95, fol.223v
45 *Wedding of Arthur and Guinevere* from Caxton's Malory *Morte d'Arthur*
46 Cameron Collection. Herbert Cole: *King Arthur's dream*
47 AKG London/Romer, Kaisersaal, Frankfurt. Philipp Veit: Charlemagne, 1843
48l Peter Newark's Historical Pictures. Bayeux Tapestry, *William and his Barons at a Feast*
48r ET Archive. King Henry II
50 Mansell Collection. Gustave Doré: *Vivien and Merlin* from Tennyson's *Idylls of the King*
52 Collections/Brian Shuel. Stonehenge
53 British Library, London. *Merlin erecting Stonehenge*, MS Egerton 3028 f. 30r
54 Collections/Roy Stedall-Humphryes. Tintagel Castle, Cornwall
55t British Library, London. *Uther Pendragon and Merlin watched by Igraine* from Peter Langtoft's *Chronicle of England*, MS Royal 20 AII f.3v
55b William Russell Flint: *"Then the king was sworn upon the four evangelists"*
56t Aubrey Beardsley: *Merlin taketh the child Arthur into his keeping*
56b Bodleian Library, Oxford. Illuminated page from Geoffrey of Monmouth's *Prophetiae Merlini* MS Bodley 623 ff.55v-56
57 © Alan Lee
58 Arthur Rackham: *Odin and Brunhilda* from Wagner's *The Rhinegold and The Valkyrie*
59 Bridgeman Art Library /Royal Library, Copenhagen. *Odin, the Norse God with his two Crows Hugin (thought) and Munin (memory)*
60 Orion/Warner Bros (Kobal Collection). Still from *Excalibur*
61 © Alan Lee
62 Bridgeman Art Library/Birmingham City Museums & Art Gallery. Anthony FA Sandys: *Morgan le Fay*
64t Bridgeman Art Library/Whitford & Hughes, London. William Bell Scott, *Lamentation of King Arthur*
64b Bridgeman Art Library/Lambeth Palace Library. *Monk (author) seated in a canopied Chair with a Book and a Desk*, Guillaume Digulleville, *Pelerinage de l'ame*, 15th cent. Ms 326 f. 2v
65 Jean-Loup Charmet. Bombled: *Knights Templer* from Jules Nichelet's *Une Èdition populaire de l'histoire de France*, c.1900
66 Arthur Rackham: *The Questing Beaste* from *The Romance of King Arthur*
68 Arthur Rackham: *Brunhilda* from Wagner's *The Rhinegold and The Valkyrie*
69 Mary Evans Picture Library. Arthur Rackham: *The Norns (fates)* from Wagner's *Gotterdammerung*
70 Aubrey Beardsley: *Lady of the Lake telleth Arthur of the sword Excalibur*
71 Bridgeman Art Library/Private Collection. Frank Cadogan Cowper's *La Belle Dame Sans Merci* 1926 © DACS 1995
73 Aubrey Beardsley: *Arthur and the Strange Mantle* from Malory
74t © King Arthur's Great Hall, Tintagel. William Hatherell: *King Arthur being offered the Sword Excalibur by the Lady of the Lake*
74b Walter Crane: *King Arthur asks the Lady of the Lake for the Sword Excalibur*
75 Bridgeman Art Library/ Guildhall Art Gallery, Corporation of London. Sir John Gilbert: *The Enchanted Forest*, 1886
76 Bridgeman Art Library/V&A Museum, London. Sir Edward Coley Burne-Jones: *Merlin & Ninnue* from Malory's *Morte d'Arthur*, 1861

77 Arthur Rackham: *Merlin and Vivien* from *The Romance of King Arthur*
78 Fine Art Photographic Ltd. Sir Edward Coley Burne-Jones: *The Mirror of Venus*
79l English Heritage/Clayton Collection. *Relief to Water Goddess Coventina*, Carrawburgh, Northumberland, 2nd-3rd cent.
79r Mary Evans Picture Library. Arthur Rackham: *Water Spirits (Rhinemaidens)* from Wagner's *Gotterdammerung*
81 Bridgeman Art Library/Hessisches Landesmuseum, Darmstadt. John William Waterhouse: *La Belle Dame Sans Merci*, 1893
83 Bridgeman Art Library/City of Edinburgh Museums and Art Galleries. John Can Duncan: *The Taking of Excalibur*
84t Rowland Wheelwright: *The King asked her whose Sword it was*
84b ET Archive/Oldsaksammlung, Oslo Carved wooden panel from Hylestad stave church doorway, 12th cent.
85 Arthur Rackham: *Arthur wielding Excalibur in Battle* from *The Romance of King Arthur*
86t Ancient Art & Architecture. *Thetis hands New Arms to her Son Achilles*
86b Fine Art Photographic Library. Jan Breughel *The Elements: Fire (Venus at the Forge of Vulcan)*
87 Arthur Rackham: *Valkyrie* from Wagner's *The Rhinegold and The Valkyrie*
88 Walter Crane: *Sir Bedevere casts the sword Excalibur into the Lake*
90-91 © Simon Marsden Dozmary Pool, Bodmin Moor, Cornwall
92 © Alan Lee
94 Arthur Rackham: *Knights hanging from a Tree* from *The Romance of King Arthur*
95 Arthur Rackham: *How Beaumains defeated the Red Knight and always the damosel spake many foul words unto him* from *The Romance of King Arthur*
96 Mary Evans Picture Library
97 © Alan Lee
98 Bridgeman Art Library/Bibliothéque Nationale, Paris. *The Round Table and the Holy Grail*, Gaultier Map Livre de Messire Lancelot, 1470, Ms. Fr. 112 f.5
99t Mary Evans Picture Library. Stephen Reid: *Finn hears the fairy harp* from *The High Deeds of Finn* 1910 -
99c Walter Crane: *Sir Galahad brought to the court of King Arthur*
100 Mick Sharp. *Green Man - roof boss from south end of eastern cloister walk, Norwich Cathedral.*
101 Bridgeman Art Library/British Library, London. Pearl's *The Headless Green Knight* in Arthur's Hall, late 14th cent. MS Cott Nero A X f.94v
103 William Russell Flint: *Ah Sir Bors, gentle Knight have mercy on us all*
105 Bodleian Library, Oxford. *Tournament*
106 Arthur Rackham: *Morgan le Fay stealing Excalibur's Sheath* from *The Romance of King Arthur*
107 Fine Art Photographic Library/© Mrs A Baird Murray. Annie French: *The Castle on the Hill*
108 AKG London/Bibliotheque Nationale, Paris. *Lancelot kisses Guinevere*, from Gautier Moab's, *Lancelot du lac, la queste de St Gral, la mort diArthur*, Ms Francais 118, f.219v
109 Bridgeman Art Library/Phillips Auctioneers, London. Herbert James Draper, *Lancelot and Guinevere*
111 Howard Pyle/Dover Books. *Sir Mador begs for his Life* from Howard Pyle's *The Story of The Grail and the Passing of King Arthur*
112 Bridgeman Art Library/Tate Gallery, London. William Morris Queen Guinevere
113 Bridgeman Art Library/The De Morgan Foundation, London. Evelyn de Morgan: *Queen Eleanor and Fair Rosamund*

114t ET Archive/Biblioteca Estense, Modena. *Troubador from March, Spring, Breviary of Henry I of Este* f.2v (15th cent.)
114b Bridgeman Art Library/Staatliche Museen Preussischer Kultur Besitz, Berlin. Casper von Regensburg: *The Power of Lady Love, An Allegorical Description of the Power of Women over Men's hearts* 15th cent.
115 Bridgeman Art Library/Bibliothéque Nationale, Paris. *Lancelot crosses the Sword Bridge, he then fights the Lions and finally Meleagant*, from *Roman de Lancelot du lac*, MS Fr. 122 f.1 (1344)
116 Hulton Deutsch/Julia Margaret Cameron. *The Parting of Sir Launcelot and Queen Guinevere* from Illustrations to Tennyson's *Idylls of the King and Other Poems*, 1875
117 Aubrey Beardsley: *Guinevere at Almesbury*
118 Bridgeman Art Library/ Whitford & Hughes, London. Marianne Stokes:*Tristram*
119 Arthur Rackham: *How Sir Lancelot fought with a fiendly dragon* from *The Romance of King Arthur*
120 Fine Art Photographic Library. John Atkinson Grimshaw: *The Lady of Shalott*
121 William Russell Flint: *Then Sir Launcelot saw her visage*
122 Bridgeman Art Library/Giraudon/Musée Condé, Chantilly. *The Round Table and the Holy Grail* from *Tristram* Book III f.1
123 William Russell Flint: *Angel with Holy Grail*
124 ET Archive. *Mass of Josephus son of Joseph of Arimathea with Jesus in Grail* from *Li Queste del S. Graal*, c.1351, French
125 National Museum of Ireland, Dublin. Ardagh Chalice
126 © Alan Lee
127 Fine Art Photographic Library Ltd. Sir Joseph Noel Paton: *Sir Galahad and his Angel*, 1884
129 Arthur Rackham: *Arthur draws the sword from the stone* from *The Romance of King Arthur*
130 AKG London/Schloss Neuschwanstein. Ferdinand Piloty: *Percival fails to ask the King the Question* from Wolfram von Eschenbach's *Die Parzifalsage*
131 © King Arthur's Great Halls, Tintagel. William Hatherell's *Sir Lancelot refused the Sight of the Sangreal*
132-3 Private Collection and Christie's. Sir Edward Coley Burne-Jones: *The Attaining of the Holy Grail by Sir Galahad, Sir Bors and Sir Percival* from the *Quest for the Holy Grail* series 1898-9 made by A Morris & Co, now in 4 pieces
134 Catherine Donaldson: *Arthur sees Mordred at the Last Battle*
136t William Russell Flint: *How Sir Lancelot rescued the Queen from the fire*
136b Mansell Collection/© King Arthur's Great Hall, Tintagel. William Hatherell: *The Rescue of Queen Guinevere from the Fire by Sir Launcelot*
137 Mansell Collection/© King Arthur's Great Hall, Tintagel. William Hatherell: *The Battle between King Arthur and Sir Mordred*
138 Arthur Rackham: *The Last Battle* from *The Romance of King Arthur*
139 Catherine Donaldon: *Arthur taken to Avalon*
140 Bridgeman Art Library/British Library, London. *Arthur fights the Emperor Lucius*, from *Romances in French Verse*, 14th cent., Eg 3028 f.51
141 Mary Evans Picture Library
142 Bridgeman Art Library/British Library, London. *Arthur mortally wounded* from *Roman de Lancelot*, French MS, c.1470, Add 10294 f.93
143 Mansell Collection. Richard III at the Battle of Bosworth Fields
144 Aubrey Beardsley: *Sir Bedevere throws Excalibur in the Lake*
145 Fine Art Photographic Library. John Mulcaster Carrick: *Morte d'Arthur*, 1862
146 Bridgeman Art Library/The Maas Gallery, London. James Archer *The Death of King Arthur*.

148 Bridgeman Art Library/Giraudon/Musée Condé, Chantilly. *Two knights in Combat* from *Chronicle of Bertrand of Gueselin:The Story of Ogier the Dane*, PEC7923
149 Mary Evans Picture Library, Arthur Rackham: *The Hesperides and the Golden Apples from Comus*
150-1 Fine Art Photographic Ltd. Sir Edward Coley Burne-Jones: *The Sleep of King Arthur in Avalon*, 1894
151t Bridgeman Art Library/Museo de Arte, Ponce, Puerto Rico. Sir Edward Coley Burne-Jones: *Arthur in Avalon*, 1881-98 (detail)
152 Mick Sharp: *Arthur's burial chamber*, Cefn Bryn, Reynoldston, Gower, W Glamorgan
153 © Simon McBride/Comstock. Glastonbury Tor & Dyke, Somerset
154-5 © Alan Lee
156 Bridgeman Art Library/Museo de Arte, Ponce, Puerto Rico. Sir Edward Coley Burne-Jones: *Arthur in Avalon*, 1881-98 (detail)
158 Mary Evans Picture Library. Willy Pogamy: *Parsifal with Spear, the Grail and the Dove*, 1912
159 ET Archive/British Museum. *Richard I and Saldin*, Luttrell Psalter, English, before 1340
160 Bridgeman Art Library/Christopher Wood Gallery, London. Sir John Gilbert: *The Field of the Cloth of Gold*
161 Bridgeman Art Library/Private Collection. Frank Moss Bennett: *Queen Elizabeth I in Court*
162 ET Archive/Burnley Art Gallery. Ernest Croft: *Cromwell at the Head of his Troops after Marston Moor*
163 ET Archive/V & A Museum. M&N Hanhart: music sheet *Queen Victoria and Prince Albert Dancing the Polka*, Julien's Celebrated Polkas No 9
164 Giancarlo Costa/Wagner Museum, Bayreuth. Heinrion: *Parsifal at the castle of the Grail*
165 Arthur Rackham: *Knight* from *The Romance of King Arthur*

Catherine Donaldon illustrations from Malory *The Death of King Arthur*, © Macmillan General Books Ltd 1928
Sir William Russell Flint from Malory's *Morte d'Arthur*, Medici Society, 1927, by courtesy and © of Mrs S M Russell Flint
Arthur Rackham illustrations, including chapter heading motifs from *The Romance of King Arthur* Macmillan General Books Ltd, 1917, Wagner *The Rhinegold & The Valkyrie*, William Heinemann, 1920, Wagner *Siegfried & Gotterdammerung*, William Heinemann by courtesy and © of Ms Viv Peto

Aubrey Beardsley illustrations from Malory's *Morte d'Arthur*, Dent, 1909
Walter Crane illustrations from Henry Gilbert *The Knights of the Round Table*, TC & EC Jack Ltd, c.1920
Rowland Wheelwright illustration from Eleanor C Price *The Adventures of King Arthur*, J Coker & Co, 1931

The Author and Publisher would like to thank Alan Lee for granting permission to use his illustrations in this book.

Publishing Director Frances Gertler
Art Director Tim Foster

Editors Erica Marcus, Kara Hattersley-Smith

Picture Research Julia Ruxton
Indexer Hilary Bird

Reprographics Manager David Blundell
Image Processors Eddie Jackson, Jonathon Drury